Letts
and
LONSDALE

Revise
KS3

French
includes audio CD

Julie Adams

Contents

French at Key Stage 3

Introduction to Key Stage 3 French

This book is designed for you to use at home to support your study at school. The topics covered in each chapter meet the requirements of the National Curriculum for Modern Foreign Languages (MFL) at Key Stage 3 (KS3).

All pupils must learn to understand and use French in a variety of contexts and situations, including:

- everyday activities
- personal and social life
- the world around us
- the world at work
- the international world.

In addition to acquiring knowledge and understanding of French, pupils must:

- develop language skills (e.g. correct pronunciation and intonation)
- develop language-learning skills (e.g. techniques for memorising words and phrases)
- develop cultural awareness (e.g. consider the culture of French-speaking countries)
- use French for real purposes, as well as creatively and imaginatively.

Attainment Targets

The Attainment Targets for French cover the following skills:

- **Listening and Responding**
  Listening for gist and detail; summarising and reporting the main points of a conversation
- **Speaking**
  Asking and answering questions; initiating and developing conversations
- **Reading and Responding**
  Skimming and scanning texts for information, including ICT and authentic materials
- **Writing**
  Producing different types of written text; redrafting writing to improve accuracy and content

The requirements of the KS3 National Strategy Framework for MFL are also addressed in the skills taught throughout the book. More information on the Framework is available online: http://www.standards.dfes.gov.uk/keystage3/respub/mflframework/foreword/

National Curriculum levels

Towards the back of this book, you will find summaries of the levels in Listening, Speaking, Reading and Writing. Use these to assess which level you are reaching when you answer the questions in the end-of-section practice test questions.

The full text of the NC levels for MFL is available online: http://www.qca.org.uk/downloads/3804_mfl_level_desc.pdf

How this book will help you

How this book is organised

This book is divided into twelve sections, each covering a different language topic. Every section includes listening, speaking, reading and writing activities to help you practise the vocabulary, grammar and skills of that topic.

At the start of each of the twelve sections is an **After studying this topic you should be able to** box, which lays out the main skills and knowledge you should have acquired by the end of that section.

Main chapters within the twelve sections start with an **Écoutez et lisez** recording, which will give you an aural and written introduction to the main parts of that topic.

At the end of each section is a **J'aime lire** reading text with an exercise and advice to help you improve your reading skills.

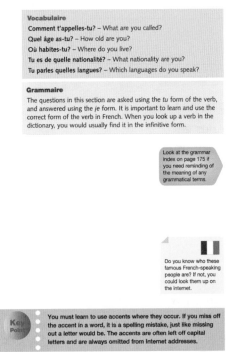

Vocabulaire boxes list the most important words and phrases in each section.

Grammaire boxes explain important language points.

Margin notes give hints on how to improve your language-learning skills, and translate any words or expressions in the text that you may not easily find in a dictionary.

Culture panels give additional interesting information on different aspects of life in France and in other French-speaking countries.

Key Point panels give exam guidance, as well as drawing attention to particularly important points in a topic.

The **headphones** symbol indicates a listening activity. The number inside the headphones indicates the track number on the CD.

At the back of the book you will also find a **Glossary** of all important vocabulary and a **Grammar index** to direct you to the places in the book where a given grammar point is covered. The **Grammar index** also gives definitions of the grammatical terms used in the book.

Using a bilingual dictionary is an essential skill for language learning and you will need a dictionary to do some of the exercises in this book.

Checking your progress

At the end of each *chapter* you will find a **Progress Check** task, to help you test yourself on the key language of that topic.

At the end of each of the twelve *sections* is a piece of annotated text which demonstrates how you could use the language in that topic to speak and write about yourself, e.g. how to gain the highest marks by using a variety of tenses. Then you will be given a chance to write your own piece on that topic. This will go into your **Dossier** of pieces about yourself. After each section are some **Practice Test Questions** to test you in all four skills – Listening, Speaking, Reading and Writing.

① Allez-y!

After studying this topic you should be able to:

- introduce and write about yourself
- ask and answer questions about name, age and where you live
- understand instructions for activities
- use accented letters in French and ask for help with spelling
- talk about the languages you know
- use French greetings

Écoutez et lisez

Salut! Je m'appelle Hassan et voilà mon site.

Je suis algérien mais j'habite à Arles en France. J'ai douze ans. Je parle français et arabe. Au collège j'apprends l'anglais, mais c'est difficile.

Envoie-moi un courriel!

Merci pour ta visite.

Écoute-moi! Clique ici.

> Envoie-moi un courriel!
> = Send me an email!

Listen to Hassan speaking about himself while reading the text in the book. Focus on the pronunciation. Afterwards, read the text aloud then listen to the recording again to check your pronunciation.

Reliez les questions et les réponses

How would Hassan answer these questions about himself? Select the correct answer from the box below.

1 Comment t'appelles-tu?
2 Quel âge as-tu?
3 Où habites-tu?
4 Tu es de quelle nationalité?
5 Tu parles quelles langues?

a J'ai douze ans.
b Je m'appelle Hassan.
c Je suis algérien.
d J'habite en France.
e Je parle français et arabe.

1.1 C'est moi!

The first thing you usually have to do when you go to a foreign country is tell people who you are, perhaps at passport control, booking in at a hotel or introducing yourself to your hosts. Use the *Vocabulaire* box opposite to help you answer the questions yourself.

Vocabulaire

Comment t'appelles-tu? – What are you called?

Quel âge as-tu? – How old are you?

Où habites-tu? – Where do you live?

Tu es de quelle nationalité? – What nationality are you?

Tu parles quelles langues? – Which languages do you speak?

J'habite	à	Londres Birmingham Manchester	en Angleterre
		Edimbourg Glasgow	en Écosse
		Cardiff Swansea	au pays de Galles
		Belfast Armagh	en Irlande du Nord

Look at the grammar index on page 175 if you need reminding of the meaning of any grammatical terms.

Grammaire

The questions in this section are asked using the *tu* form of the verb and answered using the *je* form. It is important to learn and use the correct form of the verb in French. When you look up a verb in the dictionary, you would usually find it in the infinitive form.

Infinitive	1st person singular	2nd person singular
habiter – to live	j'habite	tu habites
avoir – to have	j'ai	tu as
être – to be	je suis	tu es
parler – to speak	je parle	tu parles
s'appeller – to be called	je m'appelle	tu t'appelles

Look again at *j'habite/tu habites* and *je parle/tu parles*. Even though the endings of the verbs are different, they sound the same. *Avoir* and *être* are irregular verbs and you will be learning more about these on pages 38 and 33. *S'appeller* is a reflexive verb and these are explained in Section 6.

The **tu** form of the verb usually ends in –s and is most often used in questions.

Répondez aux questions

How would you answer these questions about yourself?

1 Comment t'appelles-tu?   *Je m'appelle Chloe*

2 Quel âge as-tu?   *J'ai 13 ons.*

3 Où habites-tu?   *J'habite à Walton*

4 Tu es de quelle nationalité?   *Je suis Anglaise*

5 Tu parles quelles langues?   *Je suis parles anglaise*

Progress Check

Match the correct answer to each question about a famous footballer.

1 Comment t'appelles-tu?   **a** J'ai trente ans.

2 Tu es de quelle nationalité?   **b** J'habite à Londres en Angleterre.

3 Quelles langues parles-tu?   **c** Je suis français.

4 Quel âge as-tu?   **d** Je m'appelle Thierry Henry.

5 Où habites-tu?   **e** Je parle français et anglais.

1d, 2c, 3e, 4a, 5b

1.2 Salut!

As in English, there are several different ways of greeting people in French, depending on how well you know them.

Vocabulaire

Salut! – Hi! (informal)

Ça va? – How are you? (informal)

Bonjour – Hello, good morning (can be used with anyone)

Enchanté – Delighted to meet you (very formal)

À plus tard – See you later (informal)

Au revoir – Goodbye (can be used with anyone)

Bonne nuit – Goodnight (can be used with anyone)

À bientôt – See you soon (can be used with anyone)

Bonne journée – Have a good day (formal)

Bonne soirée – Have a nice evening (formal)

As well as the correct greeting, it is important to use the correct form of the word for 'you' when you are talking to someone. *Tu* is used to talk to a person you know well, or to talk to a child. *Vous* is used to talk to an adult, or any group of two or more people.

The questions you learnt in Chapter 1.1 would be fine for getting to know someone of your own age, but if you were speaking to an adult, you would have to use the *vous* form of the verb in each sentence:

The **vous** form usually ends in **-ez**. If you see a word ending in **-ez**, it is likely that you are looking at the **vous** form of a verb.

Quel âge avez-vous? Careful! It would not usually be polite to ask an adult this question!

2nd person singular	2nd person plural
Comment t'appelles-tu?	Comment vous appelez-vous?
Quel âge as-tu?	Quel âge avez-vous?
Où habites-tu?	Où habitez-vous?
Tu es de quelle nationalité?	Vous êtes de quelle nationalité?
Tu parles quelles langues?	Vous parlez quelles langues?

Écoutez et cochez

Listen to these people asking questions and decide whether they are using the *tu* form or the *vous* form. Tick the correct column. The first one has been done as an example.

le flamand = Flemish, one of the two official languages of Belgium.

	Tu	Vous
Exemple	✔	
1	√	
2		√
3		√
4	√	
5	√	
6		√

Progress Check

Here is a famous character talking about himself. What were the questions?

1 Je suis belge. *Vous êtes de quelle nationalité?*

2 Je parle français, anglais et flamand. *Vous parler quelles langues*

3 J'habite à Londres en Angleterre. *Où habiter-vous?*

4 Je m'appelle Monsieur Hercule Poirot. *Comment vous appeller-vous?*

1 Vous êtes de quelle nationalité?
2 Quelles langues parlez-vous?
3 Où habitez-vous?
4 Comment vous appelez-vous?

1.3 Écoute-moi!

If you give someone an order, you use the **imperative** form of the verb. You have probably heard your teacher use instructions like this in the classroom:

Écoutez la cassette – Listen to the cassette
Levez la main – Raise your hand
Ouvrez vos livres – Open your books

In his website (see page 6) Hassan is being friendly and informal, so he uses the *tu* form of the imperative:

Écoute-moi – Listen to me
Clique ici – Click here
Envoie-moi un courriel – Send me an email

Hassan could also have used the *vous* form of the imperative:

Écoute**z**-moi – Listen to me
Clique**z** ici – Click here
Envoy**ez**-moi un courriel – Send me an email

> The title of this chapter is also an imperative: *Allez-y!* – Off you go!

The *vous* form of the imperative is the same as the *vous* form of the present tense without *vous*, so it usually ends in *-ez*. As with all verbs, however, there are irregular forms which you need to learn to recognise:

dites – say
faites – do

In this book you will see the *vous* form of the imperative used for instructions in the activities:

Vocabulaire

cherchez – look for	**parlez** – speak
choisissez – choose	**rangez** – sort
cochez – tick	**recopiez** – copy
complétez – complete	**réécoutez** – listen again
devinez – guess	**reliez** – match
dites – say	**répondez** – answer
écoutez – listen	**soulignez** – underline
écrivez – write	**traduisez** – translate
lisez – read	**trouvez** – find
notez – note, write	**vérifiez** – check

Cherchez dans le dictionnaire

You will need other words to understand instructions in this book, as well as imperatives. Use your dictionary to find the English for these nouns:

le dictionnaire _the dictionary_   la page _the page_
la faute _____   la phrase _the sentence_
la feuille _____   la réponse _the answer_
le mot _the word_   la traduction _the translation_
le nom _the name_   le verbe _the verb_

Match the French instructions with the correct English translation.

> **Progress**
> **Check**

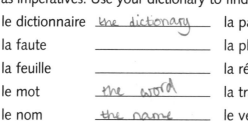

1 Écrivez la traduction.   **a** Answer the questions.
2 Écoutez les mots.   **b** Copy the sentences.
3 Recopiez les phrases.   **c** Listen to the words.
4 Repondez aux questions.   **d** True or false?
5 Vrai ou faux?   **e** Write the translation.

1e, 2c, 3b, 4a, 5d

1.4 Un accent français?

Écoutez et répétez

To be a successful language learner you need to know the individual letters to understand spelling and to help you pronounce correctly.

Listen to the alphabet and repeat after each group of letters.

ABCDE   FGHIJ   KLMNO   PQRST   UVW   XYZ

Écoutez et lisez

Five different accents are used with the French alphabet. It is important to know how accents change the sound of the letters, so that you get pronunciation right.

Un accent aigu:	écouter, préféré, général, éléphant
Un accent grave:	à, frère, zèbre, où
Un accent circonflexe:	gâteau, peut-être, île, hôtel, bûche
Un accent tréma:	naïve, Noël
Une cédille:	français, garçon, leçon
Un digramme:	sœur, bœuf

> You can find the meaning of all these words in the glossary.

> When you see an é at the beginning of a French word, or a circumflex, it sometimes indicates that the English equivalent of that word has an 's' instead of the accented letter:
>
> étudiant – student
> état – state
> épinards – spinach
> école – school
> étranger – stranger
> hôpital – hospital
> côte – coast
> fête – feast, festival
> forêt – forest
> huître – oyster
> château – castle

⁄	*L'accent aigu* can only be used with the letter e: é
****	*L'accent grave* can only be used with the letters a, e and u: à, è, ù
∧	*L'accent circonflexe* can be used with all five vowels: â, ê, î, ô, û
▪▪	*L'accent tréma* is only used over the letters e or i. It is used to show when two vowels are together and both must be pronounced: ë, ï
ς	*La cédille* is only used under the letter c. It changes a hard c (like K) into a soft c (like S) before the letters a, o or u: ça, ço, çu
œ	*Le digramme* is only used when the letters o and e appear together and are combined into the symbol œ

Cherchez le digramme

The *digramme* **œ** is used several times in this book. List the words below every time you see them.

<u> Sœur   bœuf </u>

_____

_____

French children often call the circumflex 'un petit chapeau' – a little hat!

Accents don't always change the sound of a word, but they can often change the meaning:

entre – (preposition) between
entré – past participle of entrer (to enter)
êtes – second person plural of être, e.g. vous êtes
étés – summers
mais – but sur – (preposition) on
maïs – corn sûr – (adjective) sure

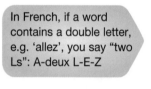

In French, if a word contains a double letter, e.g. 'allez', you say "two Ls": A-deux L-E-Z

Écoutez et écrivez

Listen to the following names being spelt and finish writing them. If you think you already know how to spell the name, you can write your answer first and then listen to the recording to check.

1 J e a n n e d'Arc
2 Z i n é d i n e Zidane
3 L'empereur N a p o l é o n
4 C é l i n e Dion
5 A s t é r i x et Obélix
6 Y v e s Saint Laurent

Do you know who these famous French-speaking people are? If not, you could look them up on the Internet.

1.5 Quelles langues parles-tu?

Écoutez et lisez

Tu parles quelles langues, Amir?

Alors, je parle français, bien sûr! Et je parle aussi l'arabe. Mes parents sont algériens. Et toi, Chloé?

Moi, je suis suisse, je parle français, allemand et italien.

Excellent!

continuez >>>

<<< continuez

Who speaks the most languages, Amir or Chloé?

Chloé speaks the most languages

For a reminder of what adjectives and agreements are, see the grammar index on page 175.

If you are telling someone your nationality, you will use an **adjective** to do this. The words used to describe nationalities and languages are similar. For example, Thierry Henry might say:

Je suis français et je parle français. – I am French and I speak French.

Note how the adjective and the language start with a small letter in French.

Adjectives in French have to **agree** with (that means, match) the noun they describe. So a French woman like Vanessa Paradis would say:

Je suis française et je parle français.

Note how the adjective describing her nationality adds an -e, but the noun for the language stays the same.

Country	Nationality (masculine)	Nationality (feminine)	Language
l'Angleterre	anglais	anglaise	anglais
l'Écosse	écossais	écossaise	gaélique
le pays de Galles	gallois	galloise	gallois
l'Irlande	irlandais	irlandaise	irlandais/gaélique
la France	français	française	français
la Belgique	belge	belge	français/flamand
le Canada	canadien	canadienne	anglais/français
la Suisse	suisse	suisse	français/allemand/ italien/romanche
l'Allemagne	allemand	allemande	allemand
l'Espagne	espagnol	espagnole	espagnol
l'Italie	italien	italienne	italien

Some of the endings on the feminine adjectives follow a different pattern. There will be more on this in Section 3. Also, make sure you select the correct language – people in Canada don't speak Canadian and people in Switzerland don't speak Swiss! The endings also affect the pronunciation. This is covered in the next listening task.

Écoutez et cochez

Listen to the list of adjectives of nationality from the table on the previous page being read aloud. Which feminine forms of the adjective are pronounced differently? Tick the correct column. The first one has been done as an example.

	Nationality (masculine/feminine)	Pronounced differently	Pronounced the same
Exemple	anglais/anglaise	✔	
1	écossais/écossaise	✓	
2	gallois/galloise	✓	
3	irlandais/irlandaise	✓	
4	français/française	✓	
5	belge/belge		✓
6	canadien/canadienne	✓	
7	suisse/suisse		✓
8	allemand/allemande	✓	
9	espagnol/espagnole	✓	
10	italien/italienne	✓	

Progress Check

Translate the following sentences into French:

1 🧍 I am Italian. _Je suis Italienne_
2 🧍 I am Spanish. _Je suis Espagnole_
3 🧍 I am Irish. _Je suis Irlandaise_
4 🧍 I am Canadian. _Je suis Canadien_
5 🧍 I am Swiss. _Je suis suisse_

1 Je suis italienne.
2 Je suis espagnole.
3 Je suis irlandaise.
4 Je suis canadien.
5 Je suis suisse.

Key Point

Success in a foreign language includes being able to handle longer texts. Before you tackle the reading text on page 15 look carefully at the two words which have been translated and the picture of the compass. You do not need to understand every word to get the correct answers, just enough to get the "gist" to put the three missing sentences into the correct order.

J'aime lire

Read the text then sort the English translation into the correct order.

Faire la bise

En France on fait souvent la bise. Les amis font la bise pour dire «bonjour».

Mais c'est combien de bisous? Ça dépend! Le plus souvent, c'est deux bises, **un bisou** à gauche, et un bisou à droite. En Provence, dans le sud de la France, c'est souvent trois bisous. À Nantes, dans le nord de la France, c'est quatre bisous.

> **Faire la bise** – to greet someone by kissing on the cheek
> **un bisou** – a kiss

In France you often greet someone with a kiss.

1 _En France on fait souvent la bise._   A

But how many kisses do you give?

2 _Mais c'est combien des bisous?_   C

Most often it is two kisses, one kiss on the left and one kiss on the right.

3 _Le plus souvent, c'est deux bises, un bisou à gauche, et un bisou à droite_   B

In Nantes, in the north of France, it's four kisses.

a Friends kiss each other to say hello.

b In Provence, in the south of France, it is often three kisses.

c That depends!

Mon dossier

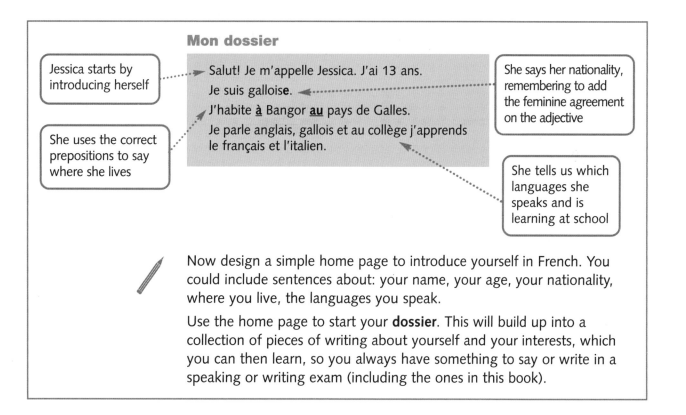

Jessica starts by introducing herself

She uses the correct prepositions to say where she lives

Salut! Je m'appelle Jessica. J'ai 13 ans.
Je suis galloise.
J'habite **à** Bangor **au** pays de Galles.
Je parle anglais, gallois et au collège j'apprends le français et l'italien.

She says her nationality, remembering to add the feminine agreement on the adjective

She tells us which languages she speaks and is learning at school

Now design a simple home page to introduce yourself in French. You could include sentences about: your name, your age, your nationality, where you live, the languages you speak.

Use the home page to start your **dossier**. This will build up into a collection of pieces of writing about yourself and your interests, which you can then learn, so you always have something to say or write in a speaking or writing exam (including the ones in this book).

Practice test questions

Listening 🎧 8

Listen to the recording and write down each person's name:

1. _Anjélique ✓_   Laurent
2. _Félix ✓_   Lambert
3. _Joëlle ✓_   Simonet
4. _Ames ✗ Anis_   Maktoun
5. _Hélène ✓_   Frézier
6. Magali _Deop ✗ Diop_   4   **(6 marks)**

Listen to the same people again, this time saying where they live. 🎧 9

Write the correct name on each country on the map.

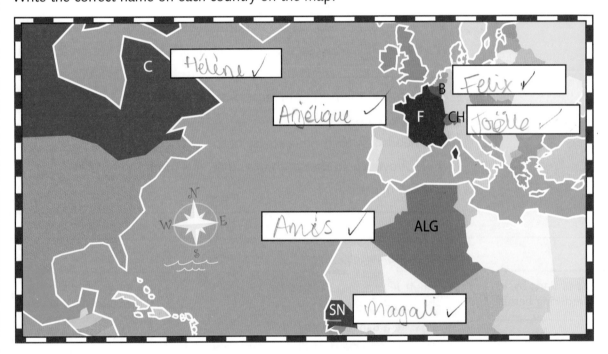

Speaking

Answer these questions about yourself in full sentences:

1. Comment t'appelles-tu? _Jé m'appelle chloe ✓_
2. Quel âge as-tu? _J'ai 13ans ✓_
3. Où habites-tu? _J'habite à ✓ Walton-on-Thames._
4. Quelle est ta nationalité? _Je suis Anglaise._
5. Tu parles quelles langues? _Je parle ✓ anglais_
6. Quelles langues apprends-tu? _Au collège ✓ J'apprends français et allemand._   6   **(6 marks)**

You are showing a French visitor, Monsieur Deniaud, around your school.
Ask him three questions about himself. (You should use the _vous_ form.)   **(3 marks)**

Où habitez vous? ✓   comment vous appellez vous?
Quel âge as-vous? ✓ (avez-vous?)   2

Reading

Match the speech bubbles to the correct speaker.

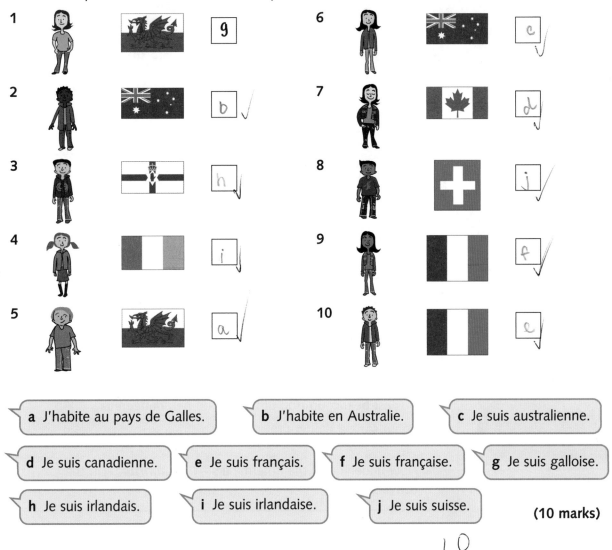

1   g

2   b ✓

3   h

4   i ✓

5   a ✓

6   c ✓

7   d ✓

8   j ✓

9   f ✓

10   e ✓

a J'habite au pays de Galles.

b J'habite en Australie.

c Je suis australienne.

d Je suis canadienne.

e Je suis français.

f Je suis française.

g Je suis galloise.

h Je suis irlandais.

i Je suis irlandaise.

j Je suis suisse.

(10 marks)

10

Writing

An English friend has asked you to help her write a short paragraph in French about her for her website. You should write in the first person singular (the *je* form). You must include:

- your friend's name and age
- where she lives and her nationality
- which languages she speaks and is learning.

Use the information on the notepad:

Bonjour! Je m'appelle Sophie Terrington
et j'ai 13 ans. Je suis Angaise et
j'habite à Norwich au Angleterre.
Je parle anglais et espagnol et
j'apprends le français!

Au revoir ✗

From: Sophie Terrington
I'm thirteen years old.
I'm English.
I live in Norwich in England.
I speak English and Spanish and I'm learning French.

$\frac{30}{32}$ ☺   8   (8 marks)

Still room to improve though!

2 Au collège

After studying this topic you should be able to:

- name the school subjects
- discuss your likes and dislikes at school
- tell the time in the 12-hour and 24-hour clock
- describe your school day
- talk about the languages spoken in some francophone countries
- compare schools

Écoutez et lisez

Salut. Qu'est-ce que tu as au collège aujourd'hui?

Bof! Le lundi on a EPS. Je déteste ça.

Tu n'aimes pas le sport? Moi, j'adore ça. J'aime le prof aussi, il est marrant.

Marrant? Il est bizarre! Moi, je préfère l'informatique. C'est intéressant.

Tu es bizarre! C'est trop facile et ennuyeux. Ma matière préférée, c'est la chimie.

Quoi? C'est beaucoup trop difficile et un peu dangereux.

C'est pour ça que j'aime ça!

Now underline all the determiners – *le/la, un/une* – in the conversation.

> C'est pour ça que j'aime ça!
> – That's why I like it!

2.1 Les matières

Grammaire

When you learn a noun in French, you must also learn what gender it is, i.e. whether it is masculine or feminine. Without this information it will be difficult to make your French accurate, as you won't know which determiner to use, *le* or *la*, *un* or *une*. The gender also tells you whether the adjective needs to add an agreement (see page 13).

Look at the following school subjects:

l'anglais – English

l'éducation civique – citizenship

l'informatique – information technology

l'histoire – history

continuez >>>

Like in English, some subjects are better known by their abbreviations:

EPS (l'éducation physique et sportive) – PE

SVT (les sciences de la vie et de la terre) – natural sciences

<<< continuez

As these nouns start with a vowel or a silent h, the article (*le* or *la*) is shortened to *l'*, so you can't tell what gender they are. When you note words like this in your vocabulary book, make a note of their gender as well:

l'anglais (m)

l'éducation civique (f)

l'informatique (f)

l'histoire (f)

Some school subjects use a plural determiner:

les maths (f) – maths

les travaux manuels (m) – practical subjects, technology

If you talk about whether you like a subject or not, you need to use the definite article:

☺ J'aime **le** français   ☹ Je n'aime pas **le** dessin

☺☺ J'adore **la** chimie   ☹☹ Je déteste **les** maths

Cherchez dans le dictionnaire

Use your dictionary to find the gender of these school subjects, whether they are masculine or feminine, *le* or *la*. Check the meaning, too, if you need reminding.

_la_ chimie   _la_ musique

_le_ dessin   _la_ théâtre

_le_ français

Écoutez et notez

Listen to the following people talking about the subjects they like or dislike. First, listen for the correct determiner: *le*, *la* or *les*. Then decide whether the person likes the subject or not. The first one has been done for you as an example.

	le ou la?	aime? ☺ n'aime pas? ☹
Exemple	**le** français	☺
1	_la_ géographie	☹☹
2	_la_ biologie	☺☺
3	_les_ sciences	☺ ½
4	_le_ musique	☹
5	_le_ technologie	☺

> You can use these expressions to talk about other things, too, such as food, the weather, your little brother, etc.

Here are some more ways to talk about which subjects you like or dislike:

Ma matière préférée, c'est le français – My favourite subject is French

Je trouve le français passionnant – I find French exciting

J'ai horreur de ça! – I loathe it (literally, 'I have a horror of it!')

Je trouve ça pénible – I find it hard work, unbearable

C'est génial! – It's great!

Ça va – It's all right

C'est affreux! – It's awful!

C'est null! – It's rubbish!

Progress Check

Decide whether these opinions are positive by putting a ☺ or a ☹ beside them.

1 L'espagnol, c'est affreux.

2 Je trouve les travaux manuels pénibles.

3 Je trouve EPS passionnant.

4 Ma matière préférée, c'est la techno.

5 Le théâtre? J'ai horreur de ça!

1 ☹ 2 ☹ 3 ☺ 4 ☺ 5 ☹

2.2 Pourquoi? Parce que ...

Justifying your opinions is important for maximising your marks: you shouldn't just say what you think of a subject; you should also say *why* you feel that way.

Vocabulaire

pourquoi – why

parce que – because

j'aime/je n'aime pas le prof – I like/I don't like the teacher

le prof est ... – the teacher is ...

sévère – strict

marrant – funny

le prof explique tout bien – the teacher explains everything well

c'est **difficile** – it's difficult

c'est compliqué – it's complicated

c'est facile – it's easy

c'est utile/inutile – it's useful/useless

c'est intéressant/ennuyeux – it's interesting/boring

> After c'est, adjectives are always masculine singular.

Coucou! – Hi there!
(to a close friend)

French children all learn to write in the same, distinctive handwriting style, known as *l'écriture*. English-speaking people often find it difficult to read.

Lisez et répondez

Read these notes that children have been passing in class, then answer the questions in English.

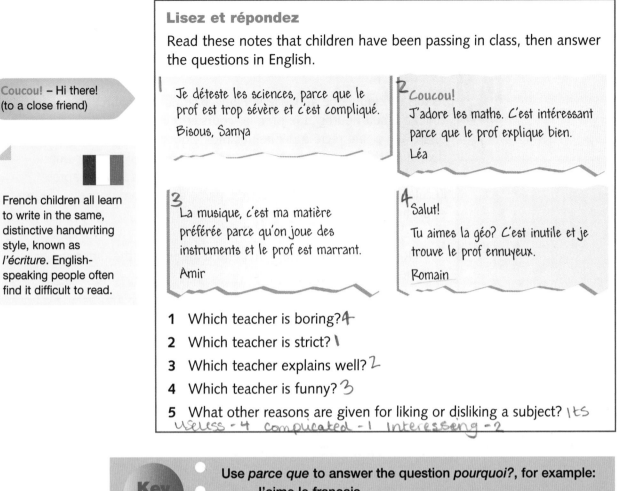

1
Je déteste les sciences, parce que le prof est trop sévère et c'est compliqué.
Bisous, Samya

2 Coucou!
J'adore les maths. C'est intéressant parce que le prof explique bien.
Léa

3
La musique, c'est ma matière préférée parce qu'on joue des instruments et le prof est marrant.
Amir

4 Salut!
Tu aimes la géo? C'est inutile et je trouve le prof ennuyeux.
Romain

1 Which teacher is boring? 4
2 Which teacher is strict? 1
3 Which teacher explains well? 2
4 Which teacher is funny? 3
5 What other reasons are given for liking or disliking a subject? Its useless - 4 complicated - 1 interesseng - 2

Key Point

Use *parce que* to answer the question *pourquoi?*, for example:
– J'aime le français.
– Pourquoi?
– Parce que le prof est marrant.

Progress Check

Translate into English the following justifications for liking or disliking something.

1 C'est inutile. It's useless
2 C'est facile. It's easy
3 Le prof est sévère. the teacher is strict
4 Le prof explique bien. the teacher explains everything well
5 C'est ennuyeux. It's boring

1 It's useless.
2 It's easy.
3 The teacher is strict.
4 The teacher explains well.
5 It's boring.

2.3 Ma journée scolaire

Écoutez et lisez

Je suis en cinquième au Collège Paul Cézanne. Le matin j'arrive au collège à <u>huit heures</u> et le premier cours commence à <u>huit heures et quart</u>. On a une récré à <u>dix heures moins quart</u>. Le lundi à <u>dix heures dix</u> j'ai maths et j'aime bien ça. Le déjeuner est à <u>midi moins quart</u>. Après le déjeuner on a géo. Le mardi on a les clubs sportifs après l'école. C'est nul. J'aime le mercredi parce qu'on commence plus tard et on finit à <u>quatorze heures quinze</u>.

✎ Now read Chloé's text again and underline all the times she mentions. ~times.

The numbers for year groups in French schools go backwards! You start secondary school in the sixth class (*en sixième*) and you end up in the first class (*en première*). There is also the *terminale,* which is the final year when students take their *baccalauréat* exams.

Vocabulaire

l'emploi du temps – timetable

le collège – school (years 7–10)

la récréation – break

je suis en sixième/cinquième/quatrième – I am in year 7/8/9

les clubs sportifs – sports clubs

le club de théâtre/d'informatique – drama/computer club

le premier cours commence à … – the first lesson starts at …

le déjeuner est à … – lunch is at …

la journée scolaire – the school day

Key Point

Days of the week in French are always masculine and start with a lower-case letter. Use the definite article *le* with the day of the week to say *on Mondays* (i.e. every Monday) – *le* lundi

Telling the time

You need to be able to talk about the time things happen at school. Look at the clock faces and revise how to tell the time.

Remember that the 24-hour clock is used more in France than in English-speaking countries, so Chloé would be more likely to say that school usually finishes at '*seize* heures' (not '*quatre* heures').

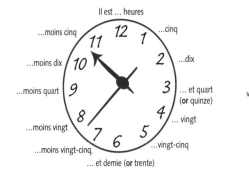

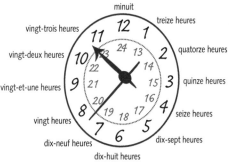

Écoutez et notez

Listen to the clock times and write them down in figures.

Exemple: Il est quinze heures quarante-cinq. **15.45**

1 Il est dix-neuf heures cinq — *19.15*

2 Il est une heure cinquante — *01.50*

3 Il est deux heures dix — *02.10*

4 Il est vingt et une heures trente — *21.30*

5 Il est treize heures quarante-trois — *13.43*

The French use *heure(s)* to say o'clock: *Il est trois heures* – It is three o'clock. This is usually shortened to *h* between the hour and minutes when you write a time in figures: 3h00.

Key Point

Earlier on page 19 you looked at how you need to use the determiner if you say you *like* or *dislike* a subject in French: J'aime *le* français, je n'aime pas *l'*anglais.

Note how when Chloé is just talking about what lessons she *has*, she leaves out the determiner, e.g. *J'ai maths; On a géo.*

Grammaire

Notice how on page 22 Chloé says 'we have geography' – *on a geo*. This literally means 'one has geography'. The *on* form is used much more in French than any other pronoun . *On* is used where in English we might say 'we', 'one', 'you', 'they', 'people', 'there is'/'there are' or even 'I'. So in this case, you could translate *on a geo* as 'we have geography', 'people have geography', 'you have geography', 'they have geography', 'there is geography' or 'I have geography'.

You use the third person singular form of the verb with *on*. This is often the same as the first person singular form that you were using in Section 1 (except for irregular verbs).

First person singular	Third person singular
je parle	on parle
j'habite	on habite
j'aime	on aime
je déteste	on déteste

Vrai, faux ou on ne sait pas?

Read sentences 1–5 below and look at Chloé's timetable. Decide whether each sentence is true or false, or not known. Look at the example – the answer is not known (*on ne sait pas* – one doesn't know/we don't know) as Chloé's timetable doesn't say what time the drama club finishes.

	lundi	mardi	mercredi	jeudi	vendredi
8h15–9h00	dessin	maths	–	EPS	anglais
9h00–9h45	anglais	espagnol	sciences	EPS	anglais
Récréation					
10h10–11h00	maths	français	anglais	travaux manuels	sciences
11h00–11h45	maths	anglais	histoire	sciences	éducation civique
11h45–12h30	géographie	histoire	maths	musique	maths
Déjeuner					
14h15–15h00	technologie	sciences	–	maths	français
15h15–16h00	espagnol	sciences	–	géographie	français
	club de théâtre	clubs sportifs		club d'informatique	

Exemple: Le club de théâtre finit à dix-huit heures   **On ne sait pas**

1 Normalement, on commence à huit heures et quart.   *Vrai*

2 Le mercredi Chloé commence à neuf heures.   *Vrai*

3 On a déjeuner à quatorze heures et demie.   *Faux*

4 Chloé a histoire le mardi et le mercredi.   *Vrai*

5 Chloé aime l'éducation civique.   *On ne sait pas*

Progress Check

Which of the following are possible translations for the sentence – *Le lundi on a EPS*.

1 Next Monday we have PSHE.
2 On Mondays they have PE.
3 I have sport every Monday.
4 We have PE on Mondays.
5 He has PE on Monday.

2, 3 and 4.

2.4 La francophonie

Richard, Canada
J'habite au Québec, la région francophone au Canada. À l'école on apprend le français et l'anglais.

Gaëlle, France
J'habite en Bretagne dans le nord de la France. Chez moi on parle breton, c'est un peu comme le gallois. Mais à l'école j'apprends le français.

Marie-Noëlle, Suisse
Chez moi je parle français, mais en Suisse on parle aussi allemand, italien et romanche.

Kai, le Viêt-nam
Chez moi on parle vietnamien, mais au collège on apprend le français et le chinois.

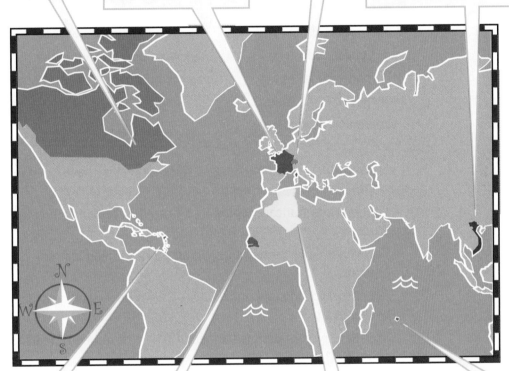

Arlette, Guadeloupe
J'habite en Guadeloupe aux Caraïbes. Chez moi on parle créole, mais au lycée on apprend le français.

Moussou, Sénégal
Chez moi on parle wolof, mais à l'école j'apprends le français.

Hassan, Algérie
Chez moi, on parle algérien, mais à l'école on apprend le français et l'arabe.

Priya, l'Île Maurice
J'habite à l'Île Maurice, une petite île dans l'océan indien. Chez moi on parle ourdou, mais la langue officielle est le français. Au collège on apprend aussi l'anglais.

Vocabulaire

la francophonie – the French-speaking world

francophone – French-speaking (adjective)

apprendre – to learn

chez moi – at my house, at home

le collège – high school/secondary school

le lycée – grammar school for years 11–13

l'école (f) – the school

Grammaire

Apprendre is an irregular verb. You need to learn irregular verbs by heart. That said, there are sometimes patterns and similarities with other verbs which can help you remember them. For example, all verbs ending in *prendre* will take the same endings; just change the prefix of each verb:

prendre (je prends) – to take, or to have, a meal/a bath/a shower

apprendre (j'**ap**prends) – to learn

comprendre (je **com**prends) – to understand

prendre – to take

je prends – I take

tu prends – you take

il prend – he takes

elle prend – she takes

on prend – one takes/we take

nous prenons – we take

vous prenez – you take

ils prennent – they take

elles prennent – they (female) take

If you want to say for how long or since when you have been learning or speaking a language, use **depuis** with the present tense:

J'apprends le français **depuis** trois ans – I have been learning French **for** three years

J'apprends l'allemand **depuis** un an – I have been learning German **for** one year

Je parle gallois **depuis** douze ans – I have been speaking Welsh **for** twelve years

Je parle espagnol **depuis** l'année 2001 – I have been speaking Spanish **since** 2001

In French, **depuis** with the present tense is used to describe things which started in the past, but which are still continuing.

Key Point

Make sure you always learn the third person singular form of every verb you meet, so you can use it with *on*. Often, this is the same as the *je* form: j'aime – on aime, je parle – on parle.

Progress Check

Translate the following sentences into English.

1 On parle français. *One speaks french*

2 J'apprends le français depuis deux ans. *I have learnt french since I was 2.*

3 Le prof explique bien et on comprend tout. *The teacher explains well and we understand it all.*

4 On prend le déjeuner à midi. *We have lunch at noon.*

5 Québec est une région francophone. *Quebec is a french speaking region*

1 We/they/one speak/s French.
2 I have been learning French for two years.
3 The teacher explains well and you/we understand everything.
4 We/They have lunch at midday.
5 Quebec is a French-speaking region.

2.5 L'école en France

You need to be able to describe differences between your life at school and life in other countries. Look at how Daniel describes his school and compares it with the school he visited in France on a school exchange:

- Je vais à l'école du lundi au vendredi.
- Mon premier cours commence à neuf heures et quart.
- On a une récré à onze heures.
- On a déjeuner à treize heures.
- Je mange à la cantine.
- Je fais du sport à l'école, par exemple le cricket, le rugby, le hockey sur gazon et le netball.

- En France on va à l'école le lundi, le mardi, le jeudi, le vendredi et le samedi.
- En France on commence à huit heures le matin.
- En France on a aussi une récré mais à dix heures.
- Mais en France on a déjeuner de midi à quatorze heures.
- Mais en France on mange souvent à la maison.
- Mais en France on fait de l'athlétisme et on joue au foot.

Use aussi to join two similar ideas and mais to contrast two different things.

Vocabulaire

je vais à l'école – I go to school

on va à l'école – they/we go to school

le matin – in the morning

je mange à la cantine – I eat in the canteen

on nettoie les salles de classe – we/they clean the classrooms

je fais du sport/mes devoirs – I do sport/my homework

on fait du sport – we/they do sport

on joue à – we play/they play

de ... à ... – from ... to ...

Senegal is a small, French-speaking country on the west coast of Africa. You will learn more about Senegal in Section 12.

Remplissez les blancs

Write about schools in Senegal. Select the correct verb from the box over the page to complete each sentence.

Mon école _s'appelle_ Lycée Cheikh Anta Diop.

Je _vais_ à l'école du lundi au vendredi. Le matin on _travaille_ les salles de classes.

J' _ai_ cours de sept heures et demie à midi.

Au Sénégal on _parle_ français et wolof.

continuez >>>

<<< continuez

On _____fait_____ de l'athlétisme.

À midi on _____mange_____ à la cantine.

L'après-midi je _____nettoie_____ à la maison. Je _____fais_____ mes devoirs.

s'appelle	fait	mange
ai	nettoie	parle
fais	travaille	vais

Progress Check

Rearrange the sentences into the correct order.

1 au à du Je l'école lundi vendredi. vais   *Je vais à l'école du ...*

2 à France l'école le Mais en on samedi. va

3 à À cantine. je la mange midi

4 devoirs. fais Après je l'école mes

5 au gazon. hockey joue On sur

1 Je vais à l'école du lundi au vendredi.
2 Mais en France on va à l'école le samedi.
3 À midi je mange à la cantine.
4 Après l'école je fais mes devoirs.
5 On joue au hockey sur gazon.

J'aime lire!

Il y a diverses écoles en France. Les enfants commencent l'école à l'âge de six ans. Ils vont à l'école primaire jusqu'à l'âge de dix ans. On peut aussi aller à l'école maternelle à l'âge de deux ans, mais ce n'est pas obligatoire.

Après l'école primaire, on va au collège. C'est pour les enfants âgés de onze à quatorze ans. Si on a des mauvaises notes, il faut redoubler. C'est-à-dire que l'on ne passe pas en classe supérieure. À la fin du collège, on passe un examen qui s'appelle le brevet des collèges.

Puis on assiste au lycée, de quinze à dix-sept ans. Au lycée, on prépare le baccalauréat, l'examen que l'on passe en dernière année de lycée, en terminale.

Trouvez le titre

Match the names in the box on the next page to the correct definition. Write the letters on the lines below.

1 School from the age of 15 to 17 _____b_____

2 School from age 11 to 14 _____c_____

3 Pre-school for children aged 2 to 5 _____d_____

4 School for children aged 6 to 10 _____e_____

5 To repeat a school year because you have poor marks _____g_____

6 Exam at age 15/16 _____f_____

7 Exam at age 17/18 _____a_____

continuez >>>

<<< continuez

a	le baccalauréat	**e**	l'école primaire
b	le brevet des collèges	**f**	le lycée
c	le collège	**g**	redoubler
d	l'école maternelle		

False friends

Although the French and English languages share many words, you need to take care not to be caught out by 'false friends'. These are French words which look the same as English words, but have very different meanings. There are several false friends in this reading task:

divers(e/es) – different, various

assister à – to attend

la note(s) – mark (in school)

une classe supérieure – the next year group up

dire – to say

rester – to stay/to remain

la terminale – the final year of secondary school
(e.g. Year 13 or Upper Sixth)

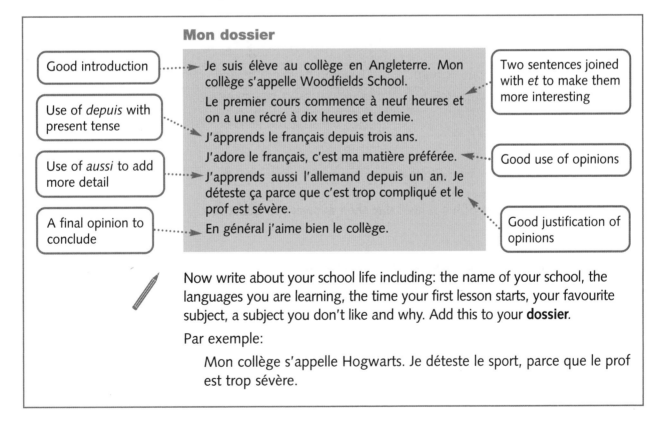

Mon dossier

Good introduction

Use of *depuis* with present tense

Use of *aussi* to add more detail

A final opinion to conclude

Je suis élève au collège en Angleterre. Mon collège s'appelle Woodfields School.
Le premier cours commence à neuf heures et on a une récré à dix heures et demie.
J'apprends le français depuis trois ans.
J'adore le français, c'est ma matière préférée.
J'apprends aussi l'allemand depuis un an. Je déteste ça parce que c'est trop compliqué et le prof est sévère.
En général j'aime bien le collège.

Two sentences joined with *et* to make them more interesting

Good use of opinions

Good justification of opinions

Now write about your school life including: the name of your school, the languages you are learning, the time your first lesson starts, your favourite subject, a subject you don't like and why. Add this to your **dossier**.

Par exemple:

Mon collège s'appelle Hogwarts. Je déteste le sport, parce que le prof est trop sévère.

Practice test questions

Listening 🎧 14

Listen to the recording and fill in the missing information on the timetable:

	lundi	mardi	mercredi	jeudi	vendredi
–9h00	sciences	français			
9h00–	sciences	français			
Récréation					
10h15–11h15		maths	sciences		français
11h15–	français	espagnol	sciences	anglais	espagnol
Déjeuner					
–15h00		travaux manuels	–	maths	
15h00–16h00	éducation civique	travaux manuels	–	géographie	
	club d'informatique			clubs sportifs	

(16 marks)

Speaking

You are talking to a French teenager about schools in England. Answer the questions in the role play in full sentences.

Bonjour.	Say hello.
Quelles langues apprends-tu?	Say you're learning French.
Qu'est-ce tu as le lundi au collège?	Say you have maths and science on Mondays.
Quelles matières tu n'aimes pas?	Say you don't like German.
Pourquoi?	Say because the teacher is strict.

(5 marks)

Reading

Read Théo's description of his school day then answer the questions.

Je m'appelle Théo et je vais au lycée depuis un an.
Je vais à l'école du lundi au vendredi. On n'a pas de cours le samedi. Le premier cours commence à huit heures et demie. On a une récré à onze heures moins quart. À midi on mange à la cantine. J'aime ça. L'après-midi les cours commencent à deux heures. On n'a pas de récré l'après-midi. J'ai cours jusqu'à cinq heures l'après-midi. Après les cours on a les clubs divers pendant une heure. Le soir je fais mes devoirs.

Complete these sentences (the first one has been done for you):

Exemple: Théo has been going to the high school for **one year** .

1 He goes to school _____5_____ days a week.
2 The first lesson starts at __8.30__ .
3 The morning break is at __10.45__ .
4 He eats in the canteen at __12.00__ .
5 The afternoon lessons start at __2.00__ .
6 School finishes at __5.00pm__ .
7 The after-school clubs last __1 hours__ .
8 He does his homework _in the evening_ **(8 marks)**

Writing

Write sentences about these people's likes and dislikes at school.
The first one has been done for you.

Exemple ☺ ÷ (teacher explains well)

J'aime les maths parce que le prof explique bien.

1 ☹☹ ♪ (teacher too strict)
Je déteste le musique pace que le prof est très sévère!

2 ☺☺ ♔ (interesting)
J'adore histoire parce que c'est interessant.

3 ☺☺ 🤸 (I like sport)
J'adore le gymnastique para que j'aime le sporty.

4 ☹☹ 🗺 (it's useless)
Je déteste le geographie parce que c'est inutile.

5 ☹ ⚛ (teacher is boring)
Je n'aime pas le sciences parce que le prof est ennuyeux.

6 ☺ ✒ (it's useful)
J'aime l'anglais parce que c'est utile.

7 ☺ 🛠 (teacher is funny)
J'aime travaux manuels parce que le prof est marrant

8 ☺ 🗼 (it's easy)
J'aime le français parce que c'est yaau! **(24 marks)**

3 Chez moi!

Écoutez et lisez

Tu t'entends bien avec ta famille, Jérémy?

Oui et non. Je m'entends assez bien avec mes parents. Mais mon frère et ma sœur, quel désastre!

quel désastre – what a disaster

Pourquoi?

Je partage une chambre avec mon frère et il est têtu et égoïste. Il ne range jamais notre chambre. Et ma sœur, elle m'énerve. Et toi, Élodie? Vous êtes combien dans ta famille?

Dans ma famille, nous sommes deux. Je suis fille unique et j'habite avec ma mère. Mon père habite avec mes grands-parents. Mes parents sont divorcés.

Et tu t'entends bien avec ta mère?

Oui, elle est gentille et drôle.

✎ Now underline all the words for family members in the text, using a dictionary if necessary. Look for cognates first (see page 175 if you need reminding about this).

3.1 La famille

Vocabulaire

la famille – family

le père/la mère – father/mother

les parents – parents

le frère/la sœur – brother/sister

le fils/la fille unique – only child

continuez >>>

<<< continuez

tu t'entends bien avec …? – do you get on well with …?

je m'entends bien/je ne m'entends pas bien
– I get on well with/I don't get on well with

drôle – funny

égoïste – selfish

gentil(le) – kind

têtu(e) – stubborn

partager – to share

il ne range jamais – he never tidies

Vous êtes combien dans votre famille? – How many people are there in your family?

Dans ma famille, nous sommes trois – There are three people in my family

il/elle m'énerve – he/she gets on my nerves

Je vous présente … – I would like to introduce …

Être is an important verb that you have already used several times in sections 1 and 2 and which Élodie and Jérémy use to describe their families on page 32. It is an irregular verb so you will need to learn it off by heart. *Être* is used so much that you need to learn all parts of it, not just the *je* and *on* forms that you would use for most verbs.

Être – to be

je suis – I am

tu es – you are

il est – he is/it is

elle est – she is/it is

on est – one is/we are

nous sommes – we are

vous êtes – you are

ils sont – they are

elles sont – they are

On page 18 you were told that it is important to learn the gender of each new noun you meet. This section shows you just how important it is, because if you don't know the gender of a noun, then you won't know the correct subject pronoun, possessive adjective and adjectival agreements.

Grammaire

Possessive adjectives are words like 'my' or 'your' that show who something belongs to. Like all adjectives in French, possessive adjectives have to agree with the gender and the number (singular or plural) of the noun they are describing.

mon frère – my brother
ma sœur – my sister
mes parents – my parents

continuez >>>

<<< continuez

The plural possessive adjective is the same regardless of the gender of the nouns it describes.

mes oncles – my uncles   **mes** tantes – my aunts

Remember, however, that the rules about the gender of determiners don't just apply when you are talking about people, but also about inanimate objects:

ma chambre – my bedroom   **mon** jardin – my garden

To say 'his', 'her' or 'its', use **son, sa, ses**. Like the other possessive adjectives, **son, sa** and **ses** all agree with what they describe, (not with the person who owns that thing) so all three can mean his, her or its, depending on the context, e.g.

Nicolas aime **son** frère – Nicolas likes **his** brother

Émilie aime **son** frère – Emily likes **her** brother

Clémentine aime **ses** frère**s** – Clémentine likes **her** brothers

	masculine singular noun	feminine singular noun	plural noun
my	mon	ma	mes
your (singular/ informal)	ton	ta	tes
his, her, its	son	sa	ses
our	notre	notre	nos
your (plural/ formal)	votre	votre	vos

NB – If the feminine begins with a vowel, then the masculine form of the possessive adjective is used, e.g. une école → mon école.

---

16 **Devinez puis vérifiez**

Work out which is the correct possessive adjective in each of these sentences, then listen to the recording to check your answers.

1 Je déteste ___mon___ frère. √

2 Je m'entends bien avec ___ma___ tante. √

3 Je partage une chambre avec ___ma___ sœur. Elle n'aime pas ___ma___ chambre.

4 ___mon___ / notre oncle habite avec ___mes___ √ grands-parents.

5 – Comment s'appelle ___ton___ école?

   – ___mon___ collège s'appelle François Mitterand.

6 Monsieur Arnaud, vous êtes combien dans ___votre___ famille? Comment s'appellent ___vos___ enfants?

Progress Check

Translate the following phrases into French, using the correct possessive adjective:

1 my timetable _mon emploi du temps_
2 my brother _mon frère_
3 our dictionary _notre dictionaire_
4 your bedroom (informal) _ta chambre_
5 your mother (formal) _votre mère_

5 votre mère
4 ta chambre
3 notre dictionnaire
2 mon frère
1 mon emploi du temps

3.2 Je vous présente ...

In Section 1, you learnt how to introduce and talk about yourself, but you might also want to talk about your friends and family. In both English and French we regularly replace names and nouns with a pronoun.

Mon frère m'énerve – **My brother** gets on my nerves

Il m'énerve – **He** gets on my nerves

When you see a verb paradigm in French, the pronouns and parts of the verb are usually laid out in this order:

Singular		Plural	
je	I	nous	we
tu	you (singular, informal)	vous	you (plural/formal)
il	he	ils	they
elle	she	elles	they (feminine plural)
on	'one' (see page 23)		

Key Point

It is important to recognise and use subject pronouns correctly so you know exactly who or what is being referred to in a sentence.

You also need to use the correct form of the verb. You have already met the first person singular (in Sections 1 and 2), the second person singular and plural (in Section 1) and the third person singular of the verb with _on_ (in Section 2). _Il_ and _elle_ take the third person singular form of the verb, so it is the same as the _on_ form.

On	Il/Elle
on parle	il/elle parle
on habite	il/elle habite
on aime	il/elle aime
on déteste	il/elle déteste
on apprend	il/elle apprend

Vrai ou faux?

Read the text, then say whether the statements below are either true or false.

Je m'appelle Olivier et je vous présente ma famille. J'ai un frère et une sœur. Mon frère s'appelle Benoît et il a dix-huit ans. Ma sœur s'appelle Clara et elle a vingt-deux ans. Elle apprend l'allemand à l'université. Elle parle français (bien sûr!), allemand et anglais.

Mon père s'appelle Michel et ma mère s'appelle Jacqueline. Je m'entends assez bien avec mes parents.

1 Olivier a deux frères. _____faux_____

2 Clara a dix-huit ans. _____faux_____

3 Clara parle anglais. _____vrai_____

4 La mère de Benoît s'appelle Jacqueline. _____vrai_____

5 Olivier aime ses parents. _____vrai_____

Grammaire

There are different ways to turn an ordinary sentence (such as 'He speaks French.') into a question (such as 'Does he speak French?').

Il parle français.

1 Change intonation:

Il parle français?

This is the most common way of asking a question in French, unless you use a question word, which you will be looking at on page 141.

2 Add *Est-ce que* to the start of the sentence:
Est-ce qu'il parle français?

3 Change the order of the verb and the subject pronoun (and add 't' if you need to separate two vowels):
Parle-t-il français?
(This is a more formal way of asking a question.)

Écoutez et notez

Listen to the following sentences and note in the table whether each is a statement (✔) or a question (**?**).

	✔ / ?
1	?
2	✔ ?
3	✔
4	?
5	✔

Key Point

It is important to recognise the different forms of questions. You cannot even start to answer in an exam unless you understand the question!

Progress Check

Match the questions and their translations.

1 Vous êtes combien dans votre famille?

2 Vous avez combien d'enfants?

3 Tu as un animal à la maison?

4 Tu partages ta chambre?

5 Tu as des frères ou des sœurs?

a Do you have any brothers or sisters?

b Do you have a pet?

c Do you share your bedroom?

d How many people are there in your family?

e How many children do you have?

1 d, 2 e, 3 b, 4 c, 5 a

3.3 Tu as un animal?

In French, as in English, a lot of nouns add an -s to the end to make them plural. If a noun has an irregular plural, the dictionary will usually show it after the noun like this:

animal -aux (*nm*) animal

the English translation

the plural ending

noun masculine

Some nouns follow a different pattern. Un cochon d'Inde (a guinea pig) literally means a 'pig of India'; note the capital letter on Inde. So when you look for its plural or gender, you look up cochon. So its plural is cochons d'Inde.

Cherchez dans le dictionnaire

Look up the plurals and meanings of the following pets in a dictionary.

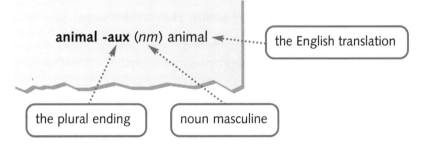

1	une araignée	s	spider
2	un chat	s	chat
3	un chien	s	dog
4	un cochon d'Inde	s	guinea pig
5	un lapin	s	rabbit
6	un oiseau	x	bird
7	un poisson	s	fish
8	un serpent	s	snake
9	une souris	?	mouse
10	une tortue	s	tortoise

You have already met some of the parts of the verb *avoir* (to have) in Section 1. Here is the whole of the present tense verb for all the subject pronouns:

Avoir – to have

j'ai – I have	**nous avons** – we have
tu as – you have	**vous avez** – you have
il a – he has	**ils ont** – they have
elle a – she has	**elles ont** – they have
on a – one has/we have	

Avoir is sometimes used in French where we would use a completely different verb in English:

Quel âge **a**-t-il? – How old **is** he?
Il **a** quinze ans – He **is** fifteen years old

15% of families in France have a pet. The favourite animal of 17% of children in France is the tiger, but the most popular pets are dogs and cats.

Traduisez les phrases

Translate the following sentences into English.

1 J'ai un animal à la maison.

   I have a pet

2 Nous avons quatre chiens.

   We have 4 dogs

3 J'ai deux souris. Elles ont trois ans.

   I have 2 mice. They are 3 years old.

4 Elle a vingt poissons.

   She has 20 fish.

5 Mon petit frère a sept lapins.

   my little brother has 7 rabbits

Key Point

Learn the main patterns of plurals in French, but also try to learn the irregular plurals of any new nouns you meet.

Progress Check

Select the correct plural ending for each of these nouns: -s / -x / (no change).

1 l'araignée s
2 l'oiseau x
3 le lapin s
4 la souris no change
5 la tortue s

5 s
4 no change
3 s
2 x
1 s

3.4 Où habites-tu?

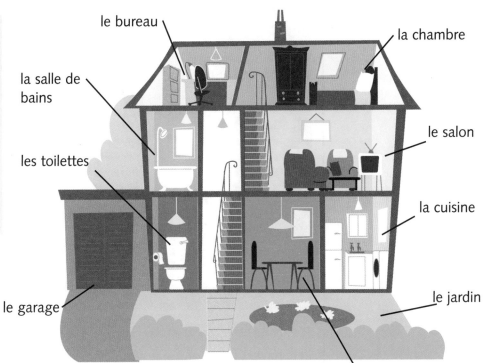

le bureau

la chambre

la salle de bains

le salon

les toilettes

la cuisine

le garage

le jardin

la salle à manger

Vocabulaire

une maison – house	**une lampe** – lamp
un appartement – flat	**des rideaux** – curtains
une ferme – farm	**une télé** – television set
un lit – bed	**à côté de** – beside, next to
une chaise – chair	**dans** – in
une table – table	**derrière** – behind
une armoire – wardrobe	**entre** – between
une commode – chest of drawers	**sous** – under
des étagères – shelves	**sur** – on

To describe the location of something, you usually need to use a preposition. Prepositions in English are words such as *in, under* and *behind*. You already met some prepositions in Section 1:

J'habite **à** Londres **en** Angleterre. – I live **in** London **in** England.

If you say I live **in** a house or flat, you use a different preposition:

J'habite **dans** une maison.

J'habite **dans** un appartment.

So the French language uses different prepositions to translate our English word 'in'. This shows that it is important to pay attention to the correct preposition when you are learning new phrases.

Remplissez les blancs

Pets have a habit of going wherever they're not supposed to! Look at where each pet is and choose the correct preposition from the box below to complete each sentence.

L'oiseau est _____sur_____ les rideaux.

Le chien est _____sous_____ le lit.

La souris est _____à côté de_____ la lampe.

Le poisson est _____sur_____ les étagères.

Le lapin est _____entre_____ l'armoire et la table.

Le chat est _____dans_____ la commode

L'arraignée est _____derrière_____ l'ordinateur.

| à côté de | sous | sur | dans | sur | derrière | entre |

Key Point

Note the correct preposition when you learn a new phrase: J'habite *en* Écosse, j'habite *au* pays de Galles, j'habite *dans* une ferme.

Progress Check

Give the French for these prepositions:

1 between *entre*

2 under *sous*

3 behind *derrière*

4 on *sur*

5 beside *à côté de*

1 entre
2 sous
3 derrière
4 sur
5 à côté de

3.5 Tu aides à la maison?

 Écoutez et lisez

Tu aides à la maison?

Normalement, oui. Par exemple, je range ma chambre et je fais la vaisselle.

Qu'est-ce que tu en penses?

Bof, ça va. Mais je déteste faire la cuisine.

Et ton frère, il aide aussi à la maison?

Non, il ne fait rien.

Il fait peut-être d'autres choses, par exemple, il lave la voiture ou il travaille dans le jardin?

Non, non et non! Il n'aide jamais. Ce n'est pas juste. Et moi, maintenant, je ne fais plus rien!

Bof, ça va – It's OK, I suppose.

Ce n'est pas juste – It's not fair

See page 105 for time expressions to say how often you do each job.

Vocabulaire

Tu aides à la maison? – Do you help at home?

Qu'est-ce que tu en penses? – What do you think about that?

J'aide à la maison – I help at home

Je n'aide pas à la maison – I don't help at home

faire le ménage – to do the housework

Mon frère ne fait rien – my brother doesn't do anything

Je range ma chambre – I tidy my bedroom

Je fais la vaisselle/les lits – I do the washing up/make the beds

Je fais les courses/la cuisine – I do the shopping/cooking

Je lave la voiture – I wash the car

Je travaille dans le jardin – I work in the garden

Grammaire

In French, most negatives consist of two parts:

ne … pas – not   ne … personne – no one

ne … rien – nothing   ne … plus – no more, no longer

ne … jamais – never

You use these negatives to make a 'sandwich' with the verb: the *ne* usually goes before the verb and the second part comes after the verb:

Je range ma chambre – I tidy my bedroom

Je **ne** range **pas** ma chambre – I do not tidy my bedroom

Je **ne** range **jamais** ma chambre – I never tidy my bedroom

Personne often appears at the beginning of the sentence, but the *ne* still goes before the verb:

Personne ne range ma chambre – No one tidies my bedroom

Reliez les phrases

Match these French sentences with their English translations:

1 Ma sœur fait le ménage. *d*

2 Personne ne fait le ménage. *e*

3 Ma sœur ne fait jamais le ménage. *b*

4 Ma sœur n'aime pas faire le ménage. *a*

5 Ma sœur ne fait plus le ménage. *c*

> a My sister doesn't like doing housework.
>
> b My sister never does the housework.
>
> c My sister isn't doing the housework any more.
>
> d My sister does the housework.
>
> e Nobody does the housework.

Key Point

Negatives can be translated into English in a variety of ways e.g. ne … plus – no longer, not any more, no more, etc.

Progress Check

Translate the following sentences into English:

1 Je ne range plus ma chambre. *I tidy my bedroom*

2 Mon frère ne fait jamais la cuisine. *My brother never does the cooking*

3 Je ne partage rien. *I don't share anything*

4 Je n'aime pas les chiens. *I don't like dogs*

5 Personne ne travaille dans le jardin. *Nobody works in the garden.*

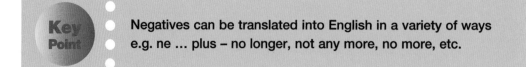

1 I am not tidying my bedroom any more.
2 My brother never does the cooking.
3 I don't share anything.
4 I don't like dogs.
5 Nobody works in the garden.

J'aime lire!

The French and English languages share many words, so a good way to tackle a long, difficult-looking text is to look first for these cognates. Underline all the words which look like English words in the text below.

Brigitte Bardot est actrice française. Elle est née en 1934 à Paris, en France. Elle habite à Saint Tropez avec son mari et ses six chiens. Elle adore les animaux et elle a une ferme avec beaucoup de chèvres, de poulets, de chevaux et d'autres animaux. Elle aime faire la cuisine, mais elle est végétarienne, bien sûr.

Elle veut aider les animaux et en 1986 elle a créé la Fondation Brigitte Bardot pour la protection de l'animal sauvage et domestique. (On peut visiter son site sur www.fondationbrigittebardot.fr.)

Elle est contre la captivité des animaux sauvages, le commerce de la fourrure, et l'expérimentation animale. En ce moment elle dénonce le massacre des phoques et le gouvernement canadien est furieux. Mais Brigitte Bardot n'a pas peur d'être choquante!

Read the text to find the correct cognate or semi-cognate to complete the English translation.

Some cognates are not obviously like English words until you read them aloud, e.g. choquant – shocking, fourrure – fur.

Brigitte Bardot is a French __*actress*__. She was born in 1934 in Paris, France. She lives in Saint Tropez with her husband and six dogs. She loves __animals__ and she has a __farm__ with lots of goats, chickens, horses and other animals. She loves cooking, but she is a __vegetarian__, of course.

She wants to help animals and in 1986 she created The Brigitte Bardot __Foundation__ for the __protection__ of wild and __domestic__ animals. (You can __visit__ her website at www.fondationbrigittebardot.fr.)

She is against the __captivity__ of wild animals, the fur trade and animal __experimentation__. At the __moment__, she is campaigning against the __massacre__ of seals and the __canadian__ __government__ is __furious__. But Brigitte Bardot is not afraid of being shocking!

Mon dossier

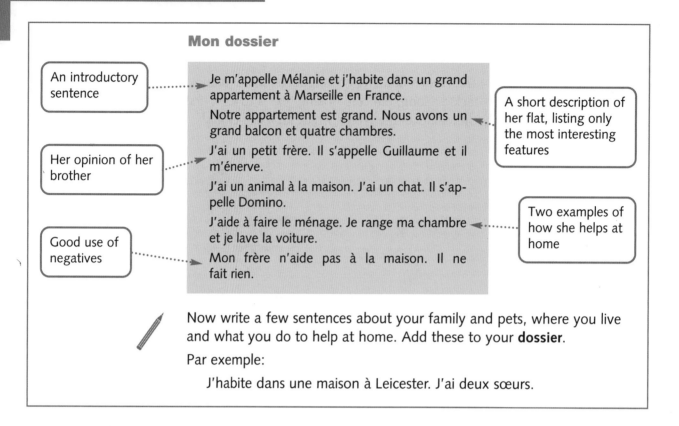

An introductory sentence

Je m'appelle Mélanie et j'habite dans un grand appartement à Marseille en France.

A short description of her flat, listing only the most interesting features

Notre appartement est grand. Nous avons un grand balcon et quatre chambres.

Her opinion of her brother

J'ai un petit frère. Il s'appelle Guillaume et il m'énerve.

J'ai un animal à la maison. J'ai un chat. Il s'appelle Domino.

Two examples of how she helps at home

J'aide à faire le ménage. Je range ma chambre et je lave la voiture.

Good use of negatives

Mon frère n'aide pas à la maison. Il ne fait rien.

Now write a few sentences about your family and pets, where you live and what you do to help at home. Add these to your **dossier**.

Par exemple:

J'habite dans une maison à Leicester. J'ai deux sœurs.

Practice test questions

Listening 🎧 19

Listen to these people talking about their families and note whether they get on well with each person or not.

	☺	☹
Exemple	sister	brother
1	dad x mother	mom x father
2	x uncle	aunty ✓
3	grandparents ✓	
4	.	sister ½ twin
5	.	brother ✓
6	.	dog ✓

8 ½   4½½   **(12 marks)**

Speaking

Answer each of these questions with a full sentence about your life at home:

1 Vous êtes combien dans votre famille? Dans ma famille, il y a 4 personnes ✓
2 Tu as un animal à la maison? Oui, j'ai un lapin, elle s'appelle Daisy ✓
3 Tu partages ta chambre? Non, je ne partage pas ma chambre ✓
4 Tu as des frères ou des sœurs? Oui, j'ai un frère. Il s'appelle Benjamin ✓
5 Tu aides à la maison? Oui, temps au temps, je range ma chambre et je ✓ lave la voiture.
6 Tu t'entends bien avec ta mère? Oui, j'adore ma mère ✓   **(6 marks)**

6

Reading

**These pets have all escaped and are hiding around the flat!
Write the name of each animal in the correct place on the plan of the flat.**

L'oiseau est dans la chambre.

Le chien est dans la cuisine.

La souris est dans la salle de bains.

Le poisson est dans le salon.

Le lapin est dans la salle à manger.

Le chat est dans le bureau.

L'araignée est dans la chambre.

(6 marks)

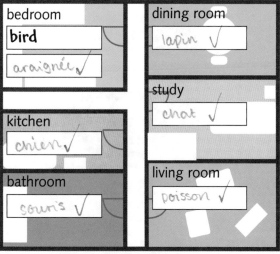

bedroom	dining room
bird	lapin ✓
araignée ✓	
	study
kitchen	chat ✓
chien ✓	
bathroom	living room
souris ✓	poisson ✓

Writing

Write a sentence saying whether you do each of these jobs at home or not.

Exemple: J'aide à la maison. **OR** Je n'aide pas à la maison.

1

Je range ma chambre.

2

Je ne fais pas la vaisselle

3

Je fais les lits

4

Je n' X Je ne fais pas les courses

5

Je fais la cuisine

6

Je lave la voiture.

7

Je ne travaille pas dans la jardin.

6

(7 marks)

4 Comment tu t'amuses?

After studying this topic you should be able to:

- describe films and say which films you like
- say what you do in your free time
- use more prepositions
- use infinitives with another verb
- invite someone to go out with you

Écoutez et lisez

Qu'est-ce que tu fais de ton temps libre?

Pas grand chose. Je joue à l'ordinateur et j'aime faire du sport. Et toi, tu aimes faire du sport?

Oui, en hiver je fais du ski et en été je joue au cricket.

Tu veux aller au cinéma ce week-end?

Qu'est-ce que c'est comme film?

C'est un film d'horreur comique. Le film est adapté d'un livre policier romantique.

Ah, je ne veux … je ne peux pas. Je veux, euh, je peux, euh, je dois aller chez le dentiste.

Aller chez le dentiste? Le samedi soir?

Oui, c'est une offre spéciale.

✎ Can you explain the joke?

> Pas grand chose – not a lot/nothing special

4.1 Qu'est-ce que c'est comme film?

If someone invites you to the cinema, you might want to find out a few more details about the film before accepting or refusing.

> Note how the adjective comes after the film in French, and how some are described with a noun: un film d'aventure – a film of adventure.

Vocabulaire

Qu'est-ce que c'est comme film? – What kind of film is it?

un film d'action – an action film

un film d'aventure – an adventure film

un film dramatique – a dramatic film

un film de guerre – a war film

un film pour enfants – a children's film

continuez >>>

<<< continuez

un film historique – an historical film

un film d'horreur – a horror film

un film policier – a detective film

un film romantique – a romantic film

un film de science-fiction – a sci-fi film

une comédie – a comedy

un dessin animé – a cartoon

c'est l'histoire de – the story is about

le film est adapté d'un livre/d'une histoire – the film is adapted from a book/story

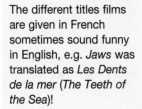

The different titles films are given in French sometimes sound funny in English, e.g. *Jaws* was translated as *Les Dents de la mer* (*The Teeth of the Sea*)!

To give a simple description of a film, say what genre of film it is and one line about the plot or the main character.

C'est un …

C'est l'histoire de …

Key Point

Qu'est-ce que c'est comme …? is a useful phrase you can use to ask about things such as books or types of sandwich.

Écoutez et notez

Listen to these people describing their favourite films. Note the genre of each film and complete the plot summary.

Exemple:

Astérix le Gaulois est ___**un dessin animé**___ .

C'est l'histoire de la guerre ___**entre**___ les gaulois et les romains.

1 *Wallace et Gromit, le mystère du lapin-garou* est ___dessin animé___.

C'est l'histoire comique des aventures d'un inventeur ___d'aventure chein___ .

2 *Charlie et la Chocolaterie* est ___pour enfants___ .

C'est l'histoire d'une fabrique magique. Le film est adapté d'un ___en français___ .

3 *Le Seigneur des Anneaux* est ___d'aventure fantastique___ .

C'est l'histoire d'un monde magique. Le film est adapté d'un ___très long___ .

4 *Le Monde de Narnia* est ___pour enfants___ .

C'est l'histoire des aventures de ___aventure a___ dans un monde magique.

continuez >>>

<<< continuez

5 *Treize à la Douzaine* est _comedie et romantique_.

C'est l'histoire de la vie chaotique d'une

douze enfant.

6 *Le Guide du Voyageur Galactique* est _comedie et science fiction_.

C'est l'histoire du voyage d'un _anglais_ dans l'espace avec

un _livre_ électronique.

Progress Check

Translate the following film genres into French:

1 a cartoon _dessin animé_

2 a horror film _film d'horreur_

3 a detective drama _film policier_

4 a romantic adventure film _film romantique d'aventure_

5 an historic film _film historique_

1 un dessin animé
2 un film d'horreur
3 un film policier
4 un film d'aventure romantique
5 un film historique

4.2 Qu'est-ce que tu fais le week-end?

Vocabulaire

Comment tu t'amuses? – What do you do for fun?

Qu'est-ce que tu fais le week-end? – What do you do at the weekend?

la danse – dancing

l'escalade – climbing

l'équitation – horse-riding

le judo – judo

la musculation – weight training

la natation – swimming

le rugby – rugby

le skate – skating/skateboarding

le ski – skiing

le sport – sport

le vélo – cycling

les randonnées – trips/outings

The verb *faire* is used to describe many hobbies and sporting activities, but note that we might translate it with a different verb in English:

Je **fais** du sport – I **do** sport

Je **fais** du rugby – I **play** rugby

Je **fais** de la natation – I **go** swimming

Every Friday evening, a huge crowd skates *(faire du roller)* across Paris. In the winter, you can ice-skate *(faire du patin à glace)* on the first level of the Eiffel Tower!

Faire is another common, important verb which is irregular, so you need to learn it off by heart:

Faire – to do, to make

je fais – I do	**nous faisons** – we do
tu fais – you do	**vous faîtes** – you do
il fait – he does	**ils font** – they do
elle fait – she does	**elles font** – they do
on fait – one does/we do	

Grammaire

The French word *de* can be translated into English in many different ways. On this occasion, after *faire* it means 'some', so *je fais de la natation* is like saying: I do some swimming. (You will learn more about the partitive article on page 113.) Sometimes *de* has to change, however, depending how it is used:

If *de* is followed by *le*, the two join to become *du*:

    le judo – Je fais **du** judo (I do judo)

    le ski – Je fais **du** ski (I go skiing)

If *de* is followed by *les*, the two join to become *des*:

    les randonnées – Je fais **des** randonnées (I go on trips)

If *de* is followed by *la* or *l'*, they do not need to change:

    la danse – Je fais **de la** danse (I dance)

    l'escalade – Je fais **de l'**escalade (I go climbing)

Traduisez en anglais

Translate the following sentences into English.

1 Le week-end, il fait de la musculation. *At the weekend I do weight lifting*
2 Elle fait du sport au collège. *She does sport at school*
3 Le samedi, ils font de l'escalade. *On saturday they do climbing*
4 Le mercredi, après l'école, elles font de l'équitation. *After school on wednesday, they do horseriding*
5 En hiver, on fait du ski. *In winter, we do skiing*
6 Moi, j'adore faire du vélo. *Me, I love doing/agoing*

Progress Check

Complete each sentence with the correct form of *de*.

1 Je fais ___de___ la natation.
2 Je fais ___du___ vélo.
3 Je fais ___du___ skate.
4 Je fais ___de___ l'escalade.
5 Je fais ___de___ la danse.

5 de
4 de
3 du
2 du
1 de

4.3 Tu joues d'un instrument?

Vocabulaire

la batterie – drums

les cartes – cards

le clavier – keyboard

les échecs – chess

le foot – football

la guitare – guitar

les jeux vidéos – video games

l'ordinateur – computer

le piano – piano

le tennis – tennis

dans un orchestre – in an orchestra

dans une groupe de musique classique/rock – in a classical music/rock group

Écoutez et notez

Listen and write down in English which activity each person does.

	Activity
1	plays on computer in the evening
2	my little brother plays video games
3	she plays football
4	plays drums
5	plays piano in orchestra
6	she plays the keyboard in a rock group

Now listen to the recording again, paying attention to the preposition used after *jouer* each time. Use *jouer **de*** if you are talking about playing a musical instrument, and use *jouer **à*** if you are talking about playing another game or sport. *De* has to change in the same way as described on page 50 if it is followed by *le*:

le clavier – Je joue **du** clavier   **la** batterie – Je joue **de** la batterie

You have already met *à* used to mean to or at a place (*J'habite **à** Paris*) and in the context of telling the time (*Ça commence **à** huit heures*). Here it is used after *jouer*, but we do not always need to translate it into English:

je joue **à** l'ordinateur – I play **on** my computer

je joue **aux** cartes – I play cards

In a similar way to *de*, the preposition *à* has to change if it is followed by a masculine or plural determiner:

le tennis – Je joue **au** tennis   **les** échecs – Je joue **aux** échecs

If *à* is followed by *la* or *l'*, it does not have to change. (You will be learning more about *à* on page 101).

Key Point

Be careful not to confuse the preposition *à* with the third person singular of the verb *avoir*: il *a* (he has).

Grammaire

Jouer is a regular -*er* verb. The endings are the same as for other -*er* verbs you have met, such as *donner* and *habiter*.

jouer – to play

je joue – I play	**nous jouons** – we play
tu joues – you play	**vous jouez** – you play
il/elle/on joue – he/she/it/one plays	**ils/elles jouent** – they play

Progress Check

Translate the following sentences into English.

1 Nous jouons aux échecs. *We play chess*

2 Elle joue aux cartes. *She plays cards*

3 Vous jouez d'un instrument? *Do you play an instrument?*

4 Ils jouent du violon dans un orchestre. *They play violin in an orchestra*

5 Je joue du clavier depuis un an. *I played keyboard for one year*

(answers, printed upside-down)
1 We play chess.
2 She plays cards.
3 Do you play an instrument?
4 They play violin in an orchestra.
5 I have been playing piano for one year.

4.4 Mes passe-temps préférés

Vocabulaire

lire – to read

collectioner les jouets/les autocollants – to collect toys/stickers

écouter de la musique – to listen to music

faire les devoirs – to do my homework

inviter des amis – to invite friends

nager – to swim

regarder la télé/les films – to watch TV/films

surfer sur Internet – to surf the Internet

téléphoner avec mes amis – to phone my friends

According to a recent survey, a third of French children spend the majority of their free time using the computer to play games, surf or email. About a quarter spend most of their time reading or watching TV.

There are so many hobbies that it is difficult to learn all the parts of all the verbs, especially if the verbs are irregular, e.g. *lire* (to read), *je lis* (I read). But you can learn to use the infinitive with a variety of structures. You have already seen *lire* used with *j'aime* at the end of each section to mean *I like to read* or *I like reading*. (In English we often translate these infinitives with a word ending in -ing.)

You can also use other opinion phrases with an infinitive in this way:

j'aime lire – I like to read

j'adore lire – I love reading

je préfère lire – I prefer reading

je n'aime pas lire – I don't like reading

je déteste lire – I hate reading

Écoutez et notez

Listen and note what each person likes doing in their free time.

	Free Time
1	collects toys
2	loves collecting stamps
3	does her homework
4	swimming
5	surfs the internet

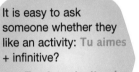

It is easy to ask someone whether they like an activity: **Tu aimes** + infinitive?

e.g. **Tu aimes inviter des amis?** Do you like inviting friends over?

Progress Check

Match each sentence with the correct translation.

1 J'aime inviter mes amis.

2 J'adore inviter mes amis.

3 Je préfère inviter mes amis.

4 Je n'aime pas inviter mes amis.

5 Je déteste inviter mes amis.

a I don't like inviting my friends round.

b I hate inviting my friends round.

c I like inviting my friends round.

d I love inviting my friends round.

e I prefer to invite my friends round.

1c, 2d, 3e, 4a, 5b

4.5 Je veux bien

Veux, peux and **dois** all come from irregular verbs: **vouloir** (to want to), **pouvoir** (to be able to) and **devoir** (to have to). The **je** and **tu** forms are the same in all three verbs, e.g. **je dois/tu dois.**

Some verbs can be used with infinitives to make useful sentences. For example, you can use the following verbs to invite someone to go out with you, and to accept or decline an invitation.

Tu **veux** … ? – Do you want …?

Oui, je **veux** bien. – Yes, I would like to.

Non, je ne **peux** pas. Je **dois** … – No, I can't. I have to …

Vocabulaire

aller au cinéma – to go to the cinema

faire les magasins – to go shopping

aller dans un café – to go to a café

aller au concert – to go to a concert

aller en ville – to go into town

aller au parc – to go to the park

sortir samedi soir – to go out on Saturday evening

venir à la fête foraine – to come to the fair

venir à une soirée – to come to a party

venir avec moi – to come with me

aller chez le dentiste – to go to the dentist

aller chez ma grand-mère – to go to my grandma's

faire du babysitting – to babysit

faire les courses – to do the shopping

faire mes devoirs – to do my homework

laver mon chien – to wash my dog

me laver les cheveux – to wash my hair

promener mon chien – to walk the dog

ranger mon tiroir à chaussettes – to tidy my sock drawer

rester à la maison – to stay at home

Écoutez et notez

Listen to Benoît inviting these girls out. He is not having much luck and they all refuse him. Note which place he invites them to and their excuse by writing the correct number into the column.

Tu veux …?		Je ne peux pas. Je dois …	
aller au cinéma	1	aller chez le dentiste	1
faire les magasins	5	aller chez ma grand-mère	
aller dans un café		faire du babysitting	3
aller au concert	2	faire les courses	7
aller en ville		faire mes devoirs	4
aller au parc	6	laver mon chien	2
sortir samedi soir	7	me laver les cheveux	6
venir à la fête foraine	3	promener mon chien	
venir à une soirée		ranger mon tiroir à chaussettes	
venir avec moi	4	rester à la maison	5

Écrivez des phrases

Use the remaining phrases to write three invitations and three refusals.

1. Tu veux aller en ville?

Je ne peux pas.
Je dois aller
chez ma grandmère.

2. Tu veux à une soirée?
Je ne peux pas.
Je dois ranger
mon tiror à
chausettes.

3. Tu veux
dans un café?
Je ne peux pas. Je dois promener mon chein.

Key Point

Learn a polite refusal (homework is always a good excuse!) and an acceptance off by heart, so you're prepared for any eventuality in an exam.

Progress Check

Match these halves of sentences:

Je dois aller — à la maison. ✓

Je dois faire — chez le dentiste. ✓

Je dois me — laver les cheveux. ✓

Je dois ranger — mes devoirs. ✓

Je dois rester — mon tiroir à chaussettes. ✓

Je dois rester à la maison.
Je dois ranger mon tiroir à chaussettes.
Je dois me laver les cheveux.
Je dois faire mes devoirs.
Je dois aller chez le dentiste.

Remember to use the reading skills you have learnt in other units, such as looking for names and cognates.

J'aime lire!

Read these descriptions of famous films (you already met them on page 48) and guess the title by skimming. Then scan the text to find the French for the English words and phrases listed below, using the context to guess the meaning.

Key Point

You do not need to understand every word of a text to find the correct answer – this is called skimming a text. You can also 'scan' the text to look for an exact piece of information, like using a telephone directory.

la lutte entre – the battle between
gagner – to win
de ses rêves – of his dreams

1 C'est l'histoire de la lutte entre le bien et le mal, mais il semble que le mal va gagner. Une jeune fille trouve une vieille armoire dans la maison de son oncle. Derrière cette armoire elle trouve un autre monde. Mais ce monde magique est très triste: c'est toujours l'hiver et jamais Noël. La jeune fille entre dans ce monde avec sa sœur et ses deux frères. Ces enfants font la connaissance d'un lion qui parle et d'autres créatures magiques.

2 C'est l'histoire de la lutte entre les humains et les lapins. Un chien intelligent habite avec un inventeur d'objets inutiles comme le pantalon mécanique. Cet homme adore le thé et le fromage et le chien aime lire le journal. Mais il y a aussi un mystère: qu'est-ce que c'est le monstre énorme?

3 Ce film est adapté d'un livre pour enfants. Un garçon habite avec sa famille pauvre. Il gagne un ticket d'or pour visiter la fabrique de ses rêves. Mais cette fabrique est dangereuse et quatre enfants ont des accidents.

these children	Ces enfants
this factory	la fabrique
this film	Ce film
this magic world	ce monde magique
this man	Cet homme
this wardrobe	cette armoire

Grammaire

Demonstrative adjectives are words like 'this', 'that', 'these' or 'those'. In French, these have to agree with the gender and the number of the noun. *Cet* is used (instead of *ce*) before masculine nouns beginning with a vowel or h:

	Masculine	Feminine
Singular	ce (cet)	cette
Plural	ces	ces

Mon dossier

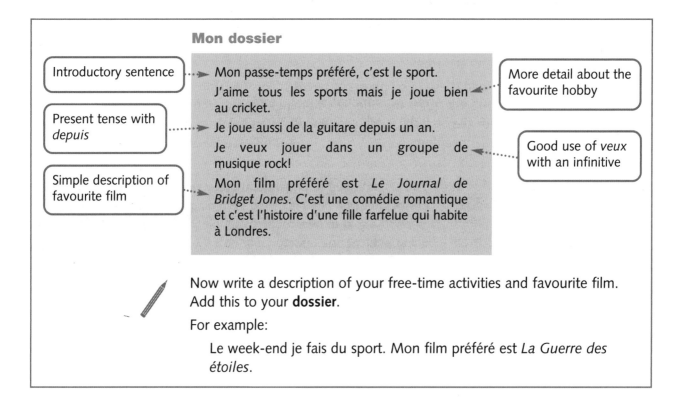

Introductory sentence

Present tense with *depuis*

Simple description of favourite film

More detail about the favourite hobby

Good use of *veux* with an infinitive

Mon passe-temps préféré, c'est le sport. J'aime tous les sports mais je joue bien au cricket. Je joue aussi de la guitare depuis un an. Je veux jouer dans un groupe de musique rock! Mon film préféré est *Le Journal de Bridget Jones*. C'est une comédie romantique et c'est l'histoire d'une fille farfelue qui habite à Londres.

Now write a description of your free-time activities and favourite film. Add this to your **dossier**.

For example:

Le week-end je fais du sport. Mon film préféré est *La Guerre des étoiles*.

Practice test questions

Listening 🎧 25

Listen to Amina describe her week and fill in her diary in English.

lundi 17	vendredi 21
visits / went to the dentist ✓	Go skating in Paris ✓
mardi 18	**samedi 22**
goes climbing ✓	plays tennis ✓
mercredi 19	**dimanche 23**
goes skiing ✓	stay at home and do homework. ✓
jeudi 20	
plays chess in a competition ✓	

(8 marks)

8

Reading

Complete the gaps in the English version of this film summary.

Ce film est adapté d'un livre pour enfants. C'est un dessin animé. C'est l'histoire d'une famille bizarre. La famille habite dans une très grande maison magique. La fille fait du vélo sur son lit. Le fils veut jouer au foot tout le temps, même dans la salle de bains! Le chien joue dans un orchestre. La grand-mère fait du babysitting, mais elle est une araignée! La mère fait du skate dans le tiroir à chaussettes. Il y a une fête foraine dans la cuisine. Mais il y a aussi un mystère – qui habite dans l'armoire?

The film has been adapted from ___a children's book___.

It is a ___cartoon.___ ✓

The story is about ___crazy / bizarre family.___ ✓ strange

The family lives ___in a big magical house___ ✓. rides her bike

The daughter ___goes cycling___ ✓ on her bed.

The son ___plays football___ ✗ ½ all the time, even in the bathroom! wants

The dog ___plays in an orchestra___ ✓.

The grandmother ___babysits___ ✓ but she is a spider.

The mother ___skates in the socks___ ✗. sock drawer ½

There is a ___fair___ ✓ in the kitchen.

But there is also ___a mystery___ ✓ – who is living in the wardrobe?

(10 marks)

9

Speaking

Answer the questions in the role play in full sentences.

Qu'est-ce que tu fais de ton temps libre?	Say you play an instrument.
Tu aimes faire du sport?	Say you do judo and swimming.
Tu veux aller au cinéma ce week-end?	Ask what kind of film it is.
C'est un film policier adapté d'un livre.	Say you have to do your homework.

(4 marks)

Writing

Write sentences about free-time activities in **each** season. Use the first person singular (the *je* form).

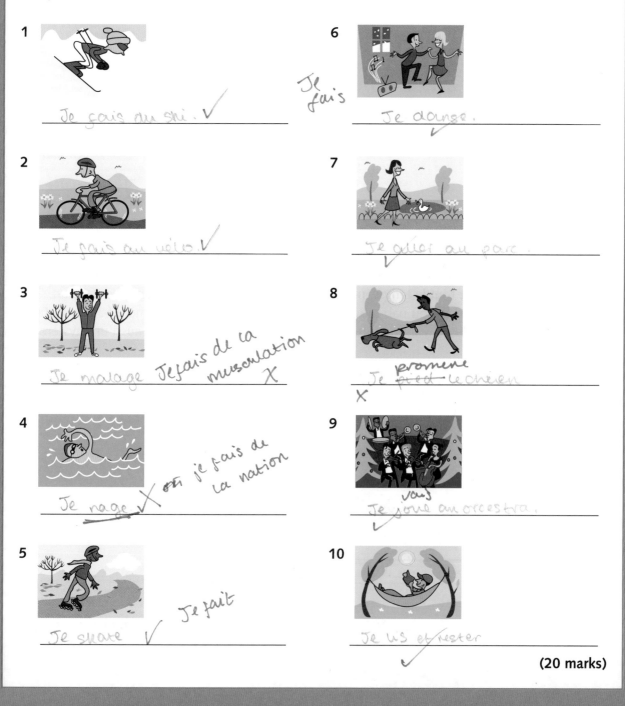

1 Je fais au ski. ✓

2 Je fais du vélo ✓

3 Je malage *Je fais de la musculation* ✗

4 Je nage ✗ *ou je fais de la nation*

5 Je skate ✓ *Je fait*

6 Je danse. ✓ *Je fais*

7 Je allai au parc. ✓

8 Je promene le chien ✗

9 Je joue au orcestra. ✓ *vous*

10 Je lis et rester ✓

(20 marks)

Vacances en France

After studying this topic you should be able to:

- talk about how you usually spend your holidays
- describe what there is to do in your local area, or another town
- talk about responsible tourism
- recognise and use third person plural verbs
- use the perfect tense with *avoir* and *être*

5.1 Qu'est-ce que tu fais pendant les vacances?

Écoutez et lisez

Je m'appelle Thomas et j'habite en Belgique. Normalement, je passe mes vacances en France avec ma famille. A Pâques on rend visite pendant quelques jours à ma grand-mère à Amiens. Je déteste ça, parce que c'est ennuyeux. On n'y fait rien. Je préférerais rester à la maison. En été je pars pendant deux semaines au bord de la mer dans le sud de la France. J'adore ça! Je vais à la plage, je fais de la natation, on fait des excursions en voiture. Quelquefois je dors dans une tente avec ma sœur et c'est chouette. Voilà mes vacances idéales!

> On n'y fait rien. – We don't do anything there.

Vocabulaire

Qu'est-ce que tu fais pendant les vacances? – What do you do in the holidays?

rendre visite à – to visit (a person)

pendant – during

pendant quelques jours – for a few days

je préférerais – I would prefer

rester à la maison – to stay at home

je pars au bord de la mer – I go to (leave for) the coast

aller à la plage – to go to the beach

faire une excursion en voiture – to go for a drive/have a trip out by car

je dors dans une tente – I sleep in a tent

c'est chouette! – it's great!

Voilà mes vacances idéales! – That's my ideal holiday

Recopiez avec la bonne phrase

Read about Thomas's holiday again and choose the correct phrase to complete each sentence. The first one has been done as an example.

1 Thomas est belge/~~suisse~~.

2 Thomas ~~s'entend bien avec~~/n'aime pas rendre visite à sa grand-mère.

3 Il ~~s'amuse bien pendant~~/n'aime pas les vacances de Pâques.

4 En été il passe deux semaines/~~reste à la maison~~ en France.

5 Il aime/~~n'aime pas~~ faire de la natation.

6 Il préférait dormir d~~ans un hôtel~~/dans une tente.

Key Point

Partir (to leave) is used a lot in French. For example, *on part en vacances* – we are going on holiday (literally, leaving on holiday); *je pars à l'école à huit heures* – I leave for school at eight o'clock

Grammaire

You have already met several patterns of verbs in the present tense including regular *-er* verbs on page 52.

It is also important to know the patterns of verbs whose infinitives end in *-ir* (such as *finir*) and *-re* (such as *prendre*).

finir – to finish

je finis – I finish

tu finis – you finish

il/elle/on finit –
he/she/it/one finishes

nous finissons – we finish

vous finissez – you finish

ils/elles finissent – they finish

attendre – to wait for

j'attends – I am waiting for

tu attends – you are waiting for

il/elle/on attend –
he/she/one is waiting for

nous attendons – we are waiting for

vous attendez – you are waiting for

ils/elles attendent –
they are waiting for

In France, lots of families go to the coast for the whole of August because it is so hot in the cities. The roads and motorways in France are always dangerously busy in the first and last few days of August!

Progress Check

Work out the correct form of the verb:

entendre (to hear)
1 on entend
2 nous entendons
3 ils entendent

choisir (to choose)
4 je choisis
5 vous choisissez

5 vous choisissez
4 je choisis
3 ils entendent
2 nous entendons
1 on entend

5.2 Qu'est-ce qu'il y a à faire?

Écoutez et soulignez

Listen and underline all the places to visit in Carcassonne.

Qu'est-ce qu'il y a à faire à Carcassonne?

Carcassonne est une ville très pittoresque. Il y a la vieille ville, où on peut visiter le château. Il y a des petites rues, où on peut prendre le déjeuner dans un café. Il y a beaucoup à voir, par exemple, la cathédrale et des musées. On peut faire des promenades dans la vieille ville. Il y a le Canal du Midi, où on peut faire des promenades en bateau. Il y a aussi la ville moderne où on peut aller à la piscine ou au théâtre.

> Be careful not to confuse où, which means 'where', and ou which means 'or'.

The Canal du Midi is a canal and series of waterways connecting the Mediterranean south coast of France with the western Atlantic coast 150 miles (240 kilometres) away.

Vocabulaire

Qu'est-ce qu'il y a à faire? – What is there to do?

pittoresque – picturesque

la vieille ville – the old town

le château – castle

on peut aller/visiter/faire – you can go/visit/do

faire une promenade – to go for a walk

faire une promenade en bateau – to go for a boat trip

It is important to be able to describe what there is to do in a place, either where you live or somewhere you visit on holiday.

See page 106 for how to say 'there is not'.

You can use *il y a* (there is/there are) to list the things you can see or do:

il y a un château

il y a le Canal du Midi

You can use *on peut* + an infinitive to say what you *can* do (you will learn more about this structure on pages 94 and 106):

on peut aller à la plage

on peut visiter le musée

on peut voir la vieille ville

on peut faire des promenades

on peut prendre le déjeuner dans un café

Regardez et décidez

Look at the symbols from the travel agency brochure and tick all the sentences that describe things you can do in Carcassonne.

a on peut aller à la plage ☐

b on peut visiter le musée ☑

c on peut voir la vieille ville ☑

d on peut faire des promenades en bateau ☑

e on peut prendre le déjeuner dans un café ☑

f on peut dormir dans une ferme ☐

g on peut visiter le château ☑

h on peut rendre visite à ta grand-mère ☐

i on peut voir la Tour Eiffel ☐

j on peut aller à la piscine ☑

k on peut dormir dans un château ☑

l on peut faire des promenades à vélo ☑

m on peut apprendre une langue ☐

Key Point

Learn how to describe the most interesting things to see and do in your town or local area, e.g. *À St Albans on peut visiter les ruines romaines.* You could be asked to describe your local area in either a speaking exam or a writing test.

Progress Check

Write five sentences about your own town or local area starting with the following sentence starters

On peut aller ... *au cinéma*

On peut visiter ... *le château de windes*

On peut faire ... *les magasins*

On peut voir ... *des monuments.*

On peut faire une promenade ... *à vélo*

5.3 Le tourisme solidaire

Écoutez et lisez

De plus en plus de touristes pensent au tourisme solidaire. Avant **leurs** vacances, ils apprennent un peu la langue locale. Quand ils arrivent, ils n'ignorent pas les différences de culture et ils participent à la vie locale. Ils demandent poliment l'autorisation pour prendre des photos. Ils pensent à l'environnement et ils utilisent les produits biodégradables. Ils achètent les produits locaux pour aider les gens.

Leur is a possessive adjective which means 'their'. Use **leur** with singular nouns and **leurs** with plural nouns. You will be meeting **leurs** used differently on page 140.

Responsible tourism (also known as ethical tourism and sustainable tourism) is a growing industry in France and the rest of Europe. Lots of people want to do more than lie on a beach and overeat during their holidays and instead try to contribute to the country they are visiting. Many tourists take part in ecological, social or archaeological projects during their visits.

Vocabulaire

le tourisme solidaire – responsible tourism

penser à – to think about

ne pas ignorer les différences de culture – not to ignore cultural differences

participer à la vie locale – to take part in local life

penser à l'environnement – to think about the environment

utiliser les produits biodégradables – to use biodegradable/eco-friendly products

acheter les produits locaux – to buy local products

Grammaire

The third person plural of most French verbs (the *ils/elles* form) usually ends in *-ent*. Listen to the text about responsible tourism again and note the pronunciation of each verb ending. The *-ent* ending is usually silent.

A few common and important verbs are irregular and have different endings:

avoir: ils/elles ont	aller: ils/elles vont
être: ils/elles sont	faire: ils/elles font

As always, you need to learn these important verbs off by heart!

Traduisez en anglais

Translate these sentences into English

1   Ils ignorent leur profs.

They ignore their teachers.

2   Elles achètent des souvenirs.

They buy souvenirs

continuez >>>

<<< continuez

3 Ils font leurs devoirs.

They do they homework.

4 Elles participent à un club de gymnastique.

They participent in gym club

5 Ils pensent à ses vacances.

They think about their holidays

6 Ils font des promenades en bateau sur le Canal du Midi.

They go on a boat a the canal du midi.

Progress Check

Translate the following verb phrases into French.

1 They live _Ils/elles habitent_

2 They like _ils/elles aiment_

3 They learn _ils/elles apprendent_

4 They speak _ils/elles parlent_

5 They have _ils/elles ont_

5 Ils/Elles ont
4 Ils/Elles parlent
3 Ils/Elles apprennent
2 Ils/Elles aiment
1 Ils/Elles habitent

5.4 Qu'est-ce que tu as fait pendant les vacances?

Écoutez et soulignez

L'année dernière j'ai passé mes vacances en France. J'ai dormi dans un hôtel à Carcassonne avec mes parents. Nous avons visité la vieille ville et quelques musées. J'ai nagé dans la piscine chaque jour. Ma mère a acheté beaucoup de vêtements. Chaque soir nous avons mangé dans un restaurant différent. J'ai beaucoup aimé Carcassonne.

Now underline all the parts of the verb *avoir* used in the text.

Vocabulaire

Qu'est-ce que tu as fait pendant les vacances? – What did you do in the holidays?

passer les vacances – to spend the holidays

j'ai beaucoup aimé – I liked very much

When you have been on holiday, you will want to be able to tell everybody what it was like. Use the perfect tense to talk about things that happened in the past (and have stopped happening). Compare the verbs used in the text above with the ones used to describe a holiday in the present tense on page 59.

The perfect tense consists of two parts. You need to use part of *avoir* or *être* (see page 38 or page 33 respectively) as an auxiliary (or 'helper') verb, and the past participle of the main verb. To form the past participle of -*er* verbs, take the infinitive and remove the -*er* ending, then add an -*é* on the end:

visit**er** ⟶ visit**é**

When you see a word ending in *é* in French, it is often a past participle, so its English translation might end in -ed. Use this as a strategy to help you when reading.

Use the past participle with the correct part of the present tense of *avoir* to show who did that action:

j'ai visité – **I have** visited

tu as visité – **you have** visited

il a visité – **he has** visited

elle a visité – **she has** visited

on a visité – **'one' has** visited

nous avons visité – **we have** visited

vous avez visité – **you have** visited

ils ont visité – **they have** visited

elles ont visité – **they have** visited

The past participle of -ir verbs usually end in -i:

dormir ⟶ dormi   partir ⟶ parti

The past participle of -re verbs usually ends in -u:

lire ⟶ lu   descendre ⟶ descendu

As always, there are exceptions to these patterns and you will need to learn these irregular past participles by heart:

faire ⟶ fait   prendre ⟶ pris

The perfect tense can be translated into English into several different ways:

j'ai fini mes devoirs –

I **have** finish**ed** my homework

I finish**ed** my homework

I **did** finish my homework (for emphasis)

Although *voyager* (to travel) sort of describes motion, it takes *avoir* as its auxiliary verb in the perfect tense: *j'ai voyagé en train* – I travelled by train.

In French, when you are describing something that you did in the past, you usually use the perfect tense. Here are some perfect tense verbs you might want to use:

j'ai fait – I did/have done

j'ai regardé – I (have) watched

j'ai écouté – I (have) listened

j'ai mangé – I ate/I have eaten

j'ai lu – I (have) read

j'ai aimé – I liked

j'ai rencontré – I (have) met

j'ai voyagé – I (have) travelled

j'ai dormi – I (have) slept

j'ai fini – I (have) finished

j'ai décidé – I (have) decided

j'ai pris – I took/have taken

j'ai acheté – I (have) bought

Remember – you can use these past participles with 'on a':

on a visité – 'one' visited, we visited, they visited, you visited …

Complétez les phrases

Insert the correct past participle to complete these sentences.

1 J'ai _mangé_ mon petit déjeuner dans un café.
2 J'ai _voyagé_ en Eurostar.
3 J'ai _fait_ une excursion en bateau sur le Canal du Midi.
4 J'ai _acheté_ un t-shirt comme souvenir.
5 J'ai _lu_ un livre intéressant.
6 J'ai _pris_ une grande glace au chocolat.
7 J'ai _regardé_ un film à la télé.
8 J'ai _écouté_ de la musique rock pendant le voyage.

Grammaire

To form the negative of a perfect tense verb, the two parts of the negative usually form a sandwich with the auxiliary verb:

j'ai nagé – I have swum/I swam

je **n**'ai **pas** nagé – I have not swum/I didn't swim

je **n**'ai **plus** mangé – I didn't eat anything else/I ate nothing more

Progress Check

Tick all the possible translations for each verb phrase

1 J'ai fait mes devoirs
   a I finished my homework ✓
   b I was doing my homework ☐
   c I did my homework ✓
   d I have done my homework ✓

2 Je n'ai pas nagé
   a I didn't swim ✓
   b I haven't swum ✓
   c I didn't want to go swimming ☐
   d I didn't go swimming ✓
   e I wasn't going swimming ☐

1 a, c, d 2 a, b, d

5.5 Où es-tu allé l'année dernière?

Écoutez et lisez

30

L'année dernière j'ai fait un échange scolaire. D'abord, à Pâques, mon correspondant anglais est venu en France pendant dix jours. Il s'appelle Oliver et il est un peu bizarre. Plus tard je suis allé en Angleterre avec mon école. Je suis arrivé en juin mais **il faisait froid et il pleuvait**

continuez >>>

<<< continuez

beaucoup. Je suis resté chez Oliver. Quel désastre! J'ai partagé une chambre avec Oliver et je n'ai pas aimé ça. On a fait des excursions, par exemple, nous sommes allés à Londres, mais Oliver est resté à la maison! Je ne me suis pas amusé chez Oliver.

✎ List (in English) all the things that the writer disliked about his school exchange.

> **il faisait froid et il pleuvait beaucoup –** it was cold and it rained a lot

[handwritten notes:] it was cold and rained a lot he had to share a bedroom with Oliver. When we went on trips, Oliver stayed at home I didn't have fun at Olivers.

Vocabulaire

Où es-tu allé l'année dernière? – Where did you go last year?

un échange scolaire – a school exchange

mon correspondant anglais est venu – my English partner came

plus tard – later

je suis resté – I stayed

nous sommes allés – we went

Oliver est resté à la maison – Oliver stayed at home

Je ne me suis pas amusé – I didn't enjoy myself

There are some verbs in French that use *être* as the auxiliary verb instead of *avoir*. These are nearly all verbs that describe movement of one kind or another:

aller – to go	partir – to leave
arriver – to arrive	rentrer – to return
descendre – to go down	sortir – to go out
entrer – to enter	tomber – to fall
monter – to climb, to go up	venir – to come

A few describe a change of state or circumstance:

rester – to stay   naître – to be born   mourir – to die

Many of these verbs have irregular past participles so you need to learn them off by heart:

je suis arrivé – I (have) arrived

je suis descendu – I went down

je suis entré – I entered/have gone in

je suis monté – I went up/have climbed

je suis parti – I (have) left

je suis sorti – I went out/have gone out

je suis tombé – I fell/have fallen

je suis venu – I came/have come

je suis resté – I (have) stayed

je suis né – I was born

il est mort – he (has) died

Grammaire

je suis allé – I went/I have gone   **nous sommes allés** – we went

tu es allé – you went   **vous êtes allés** – you went

il est allé – he went   **ils sont allés** – they went

elle est allée – she went   **elles sont allées** – they went

on est allé – we/they/you went

The past participles of *être* verbs behave like adjectives, so you have to make them agree. This means that a past participle describing an action done by a woman usually adds an -e, and past participles describing the action of a plural subject add an -s.

il est allé – he went

elle est allée – she went

ils sont allés – they went

elles sont allées – they (a group of women) went

Remplissez les blancs

Fill in the gaps in the following sentences with the correct part of *être* and the agreement on the end of the past participle.

1 Il _____ est _____ né____ en France.

2 Elles _____ sont _____ allé_es_ en Angleterre.

3 Vous _____ êtés _____ arrivé_e_ à quelle heure?

4 Elle _____ sont _____ parti_s_ à huit heures.

5 Ils _____ sont _____ tombé_s_ du vélo.

6 Nous _____ sommes _____ monté_e_ dans la tour Eiffel.

Key Point

All reflexive verbs also take **être** in the perfect tense, e.g. *je me suis amusé pendant les vacances* – I enjoyed myself during my holidays. You will learn more about this on page 80.

Progress Check

Decide whether each of these verbs takes *avoir* or *être* in the perfect tense.

1 aller *être*

2 voyager *avoir*

3 visiter *avoir*

4 partir *être*

5 venir *être*

1 être
2 avoir
3 avoir
4 être
5 être

J'aime lire!

La France touristique

La France est la destination la plus populaire pour les touristes. Chaque année, 70 millions de gens visitent la France. Mais les français passent leurs vacances en France aussi. Et pourquoi pas, parce qu'en France on a de beaux paysages, des vins connus, une cuisine délicieuse, des endroits touristiques et un climat agréable. Les gens qui habitent dans une grande ville ont souvent une maison secondaire à la campagne ou sur la côte pour profiter du bon climat. En hiver on va à la montagne pour faire du ski.

Trouvez le français

Read the text above and find the French for the following words and phrases:

1 the most popular tourist destination

la plus populaire pour les touristes

2 the French spend their holidays in France

Les français passent leurs vacances en France

3 famous wines

vin connus

4 a second home in the country

une maison secondaire à la campagne

5 to make the most of the good weather

profiter du bon climat

6 they go to the mountains

on va à la montagne

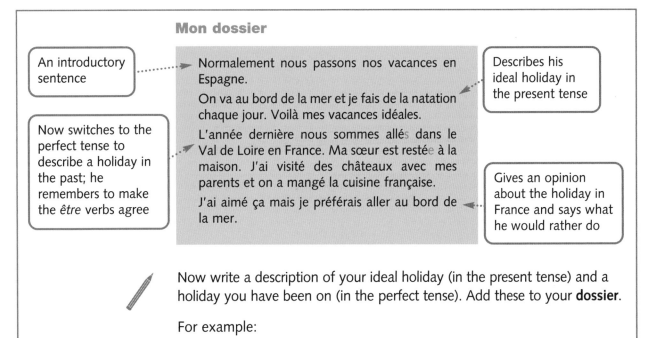

Mon dossier

An introductory sentence

Now switches to the perfect tense to describe a holiday in the past; he remembers to make the *être* verbs agree

Normalement nous passons nos vacances en Espagne.
On va au bord de la mer et je fais de la natation chaque jour. Voilà mes vacances idéales.
L'année dernière nous sommes allés dans le Val de Loire en France. Ma sœur est restée à la maison. J'ai visité des châteaux avec mes parents et on a mangé la cuisine française.
J'ai aimé ça mais je préférais aller au bord de la mer.

Describes his ideal holiday in the present tense

Gives an opinion about the holiday in France and says what he would rather do

Now write a description of your ideal holiday (in the present tense) and a holiday you have been on (in the perfect tense). Add these to your **dossier**.

For example:

L'année dernière je suis allé en Floride aux États-Unis.

Practice test questions

Listening 🎧 31

Listen to Amélie describing her weekend in Paris and note the correct number for each picture.

a **I**

b **2** ✓

c **7**

d **3** ✓

e **9** ✓

f **5** ✓

g **4** ✓

h **6** ✓

i **8** ✓

j **10**

9

(9 marks)

Speaking

Answer the questions in the role play in full sentences.

Où est-ce que tu vas pendant les vacances?
Say you usually visit your grandparents.
Où es-tu allé(e) l'année dernière en vacances?
Say last year you went to France.
Qu'est-ce que tu as fait?
Say you visited museums and castles.
Où est-ce que tu as mangé?
Say you ate in French restaurants.
Tu aimes la France?
Say yes, you had a good time.

(5 marks)

5

5

Reading

Work out which halves of these sentences about responsible tourism go together.

1 De plus en plus de touristes _pensent au tourisme solidaire._ ✓
2 Ils achètent _les produits locaux_ ✓
3 Ils apprennent _un peu de la langue locale_ ✓
4 Ils demandent poliment l'autorisation _pour prendre des photos_ ✓
5 Ils n'ignorent pas _les différences de culture_ ✓
6 Ils participent _à la vie locale._ ✓
7 Ils utilisent _les produits biodégradables_ ✓

a à la vie locale.	**e** pensent au tourisme solidaire.
b les différences de culture.	**f** pour prendre des photos.
c les produits biodégradables.	**g** un peu de la langue locale.
d les produits locaux.	

(7 marks)

Writing

Write sentences to say what you can do in the Loire Valley, using the pronoun 'on'.

On peut manger au restaurant ✓
On peut faire de la natation ✓
On peut visiter des musées ✓
On peut voir le cathedrales ✓
On peut faire du vélo ✓
On peut faire a la promenades a bâteau ✓
des

6

(6 marks)

6 Mon look

After studying this topic you should be able to:
- name different items of clothing and different colours
- say which kind of clothes you prefer
- ask for clothes in a shop
- describe your daily routine
- describe and give your opinion of your school uniform
- read an authentic poem

Écoutez et lisez

- Je préfère un look décontracté, par exemple un pantalon pattes d'éléphants et une chemise. J'aime les couleurs sombres. C'est un style branché.

- J'aime le look sport. Je mets un sweat et un pantalon de jogging chaque jour. Mon look est pratique et confortable. Tous mes vêtements sont de la marque de mon équipe de foot, les Bleus. Et ma couleur préférée, c'est bien sûr le bleu!

- J'aime le look habillé parce que c'est chic et élégant. Je me maquille chaque jour et je m'occupe de ma coiffure. Quand je m'habille, je pense beaucoup aux couleurs qui me vont. Je préfère les couleurs noir et blanc parce qu'elles sont super à la mode!

- Mon look? Je porte un jean et un sweat. S'il fait chaud, je porte un tee-shirt et un short. Voilà mon look. Les vêtements et la mode et tout ça, ça ne m'intéresse pas.

> **s'il fait chaud** – if the weather is hot
>
> **et tout ça** – and all that

✎ Now underline all the words for items of clothing.

6.1 Chacun son look

Vocabulaire

quand je m'habille – when I get dressed

les couleurs qui me vont – the colours that suit me

les vêtements (m) – clothes

la mode – fashion

à la mode – fashionable

un pantalon pattes d'éléphants – flared/boot-leg trousers

une chemise – shirt

la coiffure – hairstyle

un look décontracté – casual look

le look habillé – formal look

le look sport – sporty look

un style branché – up-to-date style, trendy look

continuez >>>

<<< continuez

sombre – muted

pratique – practical

confortable – comfy

la marque – label, brand

mon équipe de foot –
my football team

les Bleus –
the French national football team

élégant – ele

chic – smart, s

porter – to wea

mettre – to put

s'intéresser à –
to be interested in

se maquiller – to put on make up

s'occuper de – to be interested in
(take trouble with)

s'habiller – to get dressed

In the 'Écoutez et lisez' task on page 72 you saw several English loan words. These are words which have been borrowed from English or another language, e.g. *le look*. But sometimes these words are used slightly differently in French:

> Remember that all adjectives in French have to agree with the noun they are describing (see page 13).

> English borrows words from French, too! Many of our words to do with fashion and fine food are borrowed directly from French: *haute couture, chic, cuisine, gastronomie*.

un fast-food – a fast food restaurant

les fast-foods – junk food

un jean – a pair of jeans

un short – a pair of shorts
} (singular in French, plural in English)

un sweat – a sweatshirt

les chips – crisps (not chips!)

un parking – a car park

un camping – a campsite

le week-end – the weekend

Regardez et décidez

Select the correct description to match the picture below.

A Il porte toujours les vêtements élegants et il s'occupe de son look. Il porte une cravate bleue et un gilet gris. Sa coiffure est à la mode. C'est un look décontracté.

B Il préfère les couleurs sombres, mais ses vêtements ne sont pas pratiques. Il s'occupe de sa coiffure et il porte des chaussures noires. C'est un look habillé.

C Tous ses vêtements sont de la marque. Ses chaussures sont à la mode. Il porte une veste grise et un pantalon noir. Sa cravate est verte. C'est un style branché.

Grammaire

You can use several different words to say 'wear' in French:

porter – to wear, carry

s'habiller – to get dressed

mettre – to put, put on

Mettre is an irregular verb:

mettre – to put, put on

je mets	nous mettons
tu mets	vous mettez
il/elle/on met	ils/elles mettent

Every Friday, the *Galeries Lafayette* department store in Paris holds a free 'haute couture' fashion show, featuring all the latest fashions for men and women.

Key Point

Learn how to describe your favourite clothes and what you usually wear:

Je préfère les vêtements/le look …

Normalement je mets …

Progress Check

Translate the following sentences into English:

1 J'aime le look sport.

2 Je préfère les vêtements élégants.

3 Je porte un jean.

4 Je mets un sweat.

5 Je pense beaucoup à mes vêtements.

1 I like the sporty look/a sporty style.
2 I prefer elegant clothes.
3 I wear/am wearing jeans.
4 I put on/am putting on/wear a sweatshirt.
5 I think about my clothes a lot.

6.2 Au magasin de vêtements

In a French exam, you would usually be expected to know what to *say* as a customer. You only need to be able to *recognise and understand* what a shop assistant, ticket clerk, waiter, doctor or other official might say to you.

Vocabulaire

Au magasin de vêtements – in the clothes shop

Asking for something in a shop:

Je voudrais … – I would like …

Je cherche … – I am looking for …

Avez-vous …? – Do you have …?

What the shop assistant might say:

De quelle taille? – Which size?

De quelle couleur? – What colour?

Describing the item:

en laine – woollen

en coton – (made of) cotton

en cuir – (made of) leather

de taille petite/moyenne/grande – small/medium/large size

Closing the deal:

C'est trop cher/grand/petit – It's too expensive/big/small

Ça ne me va pas – It doesn't suit me

Je l'aime – I like it

Je le/la/les prends – I'll take it/them

continuez >>>

<<< continuez

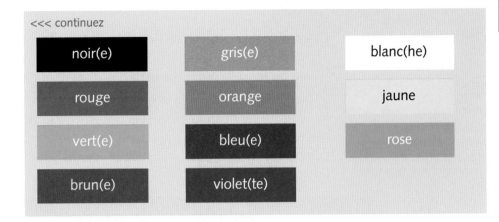

noir(e)	gris(e)	blanc(he)
rouge	orange	jaune
vert(e)	bleu(e)	rose
brun(e)	violet(te)	

Grammaire

In many sentences, the noun can be replaced by a direct object pronoun. This avoids repetition, in the same way as you might use 'it' in English:

J'aime le tee-shirt. Je prends le tee-shirt – I like the T-shirt. I'll take the T-shirt.

J'aime le tee-shirt. Je **le** prends – I like the T-shirt. I'll take **it**.

If the noun you want to replace is masculine, use *le* (like the T-shirt example above).

If the noun you want to replace is feminine, use *la*:

J'aime la jupe. Je **la** prends – I like the skirt. I'll take **it**.

If the noun you want to replace is plural, use *les*:

J'aime les baskets. Je **les** prends – I like the trainers. I'll take **them**.

The object pronoun usually comes before the verb. If the verb begins with a vowel, *le* and *la* are shortened to *l'*:

Je **l'**aime – I like it.

Écoutez et notez

Listen to the four conversations taking place in a clothes shop and note down all the details of what the customers want, and whether or not they take it.

	Looking for ...	Buys it? ✓/X
1		
2		
3		
4		

An idiom is a group of words in a fixed order that have a particular meaning different from the meanings of each word understood on its own. For example, 'to kick the bucket' in English means to die – nothing to do with buckets at all!

Idioms

Colours appear often in idioms in both French and English. The old-fashioned French expression *Sacré bleu!* literally means 'Holy blue!', but would be more sensibly translated as something like 'Good heavens!'.

Using idiomatic language makes your French sound more authentic. You have to be very careful, however, when you look up idioms in a dictionary. Never use an idiom you have tried to translate from English, as it might be completely meaningless, but stick to idioms you have learnt from your French books.

Key Point

Beware of trying to translate into French word for word. Even with the most simple phrases you will soon come unstuck. Instead you have to build a stock of useful phrases and structures which you can adapt by understanding the grammar.

Progress Check

Translate the following sentences into French:

1 I am looking for a pair of black jeans.

2 Do you have a red T-shirt?

3 I prefer the blue gloves.

4 I don't like it.

5 I like the jacket. I'll take it.

5 J'aime le blouson. Je le prends.
4 Je ne l'aime pas.
3 Je préfère les gants bleus.
2 Avez-vous un tee-shirt rouge?
1 Je cherche un jean noir.

6.3 Tu es comment?

 Écoutez et lisez

Je suis assez petite et mince. J'ai les cheveux mi-longs, bruns et raides, et les yeux verts. Je ressemble à mon frère, mais il est plus grand que moi.

Je suis très grand et mince. J'ai les cheveux courts, bruns et raides, et les yeux verts. Je ressemble à ma sœur, mais elle est moins grande que moi.

Vocabulaire

les yeux (m pl) – eyes

les cheveux (m pl) – hair

le bouton – spot

roux – red (of hair)

frisé – curly, frizzy

raide – straight (of hair)

bouclé – curly, wavy

court – short

mi-long – mid-length, shoulder length

Je suis	assez	grand(e)
Il/Elle est	très	petit(e)
	un peu	mince
		gros(se)
		sportif(-ive)
	de taille moyenne	

J'ai	les yeux	bleus
Il/Elle a		verts
		gris
		marron
	les cheveux	blonds
		bruns
		noirs
		roux
		frisés
		raides
		bouclés
		courts
		mi-longs/longs
	des boutons	

Marron, the adjective for brown or chestnut, never agrees: J'ai les yeux marron.

Je pense que je suis moche/laid(e)/joli(e) – I think I am unattractive/ugly/pretty

Je porte des lunettes/une barbe/des boucles d'oreilles – I wear glasses/a beard/earrings

Je ressemble à… – I look like…

Key Point

- For additional points in an exam, use more complex sentences.
- Join two similar ideas with *et*, e.g. J'ai les cheveux courts et blonds.
- Join contrasting points with *mais*, e.g. Je suis petite mais grosse.

Grammaire

Comparatives are used to compare people or things, e.g. I am bigger than you. Most comparatives in French consist of two words:

> plus (+ adjective) que
> moins (+ adjective) que

> Mon frère est plus grand que ma sœur – My brother is taller than my sister

> Ma sœur est moins grande que mon frère – My sister is smaller/less big than my brother

To say that things are equal, use *aussi* (+ adjective) *que*:

> Mon frère est aussi grand que mon père – My brother is as tall as my father

The adjectives in comparatives need to agree with the noun:

> Mon frère est plus grand que moi
> Ma sœur est plus grand**e** que moi

Key Point

Memorise a description of yourself (in the first person) and another person, such as your mother or your best friend (in the third person). This will come in handy in your exams.

> Pay attention to the negatives.
> André and Benoît are boys' names.
> Céline and Didi are girls' names.

C'est logique!

A logic puzzle: four friends, André, Benoît, Céline and Didi each have different taste in clothes (sporty, casual, formal and no interest), a different eye colour (black, blue, brown, green) and different hair colour (black, blond, brown and red). Read the clues below to work out which person is which and fill in the table.

Benoît n'a pas les yeux bruns.

Une fille ne s'intéresse pas aux vêtements et elle n'a pas de look.

Céline n'aime pas le look habillé.

Un garçon a des yeux verts avec les cheveux roux.

La fille avec les cheveux bruns n'a pas les yeux bleus.

André n'a pas les yeux noirs, et il n'aime pas le look habillé.

Le garçon avec les cheveux blonds n'a pas les yeux bleus.

Le garçon avec les cheveux roux n'aime pas le look sport.

La fille avec les yeux bruns a les cheveux de même couleur.

Une fille a les cheveux noirs.

André aime le look décontracté.

Didi n'a pas les cheveux noirs et elle n'aime pas le look sport.

La personne avec les cheveux noirs a les yeux d'une couleur différente.

Un garçon aime le look habillé.

continuez >>>

<<< continuez

	Yeux				Cheveux				Look			
	bleus	bruns	noirs	verts	blonds	bruns	noirs	roux	décontracté	habillé	pas de look	sport
André												
Benoît												
Céline												
Didi												

Progress Check

Translate the following sentences into French:

1 He has long, black hair.

2 He wears a beard and earrings.

3 She has shoulder-length, blond hair.

4 She wears glasses.

5 I am smaller than my father.

1 Il a les cheveux longs et noirs.
2 Il porte une barbe et des boucles d'oreilles.
3 Elle a les cheveux mi-longs et blonds.
4 Elle porte des lunettes.
5 Je suis plus petit(e)/moins grand(e) que mon père.

6.4 Ma routine le matin

35 **Écoutez et lisez**

Je me réveille à sept heures et je me lève à sept heures et quart. D'abord je me lave, puis je m'habille. Je prends mon petit déjeuner et après je me brosse les dents. Je pars à l'école à huit heures moins quart. Je rentre à la maison à quatre heures et demie et je prends mon goûter tout de suite. Je me couche à dix heures.

Now underline all the time phrases.

Le goûter is a snack French children have when they get home from school at about 4 or 5 o'clock. This is because most French families don't have dinner until 8 o'clock in the evening. It literally means 'a taste' and the snack can be sweet or savoury. Popular snacks include *une tartine au chocolat* (a few squares of dark chocolate with a piece of buttered bread), or a piece of cake with a glass of milk.

Vocabulaire

se réveiller – to wake up

se lever – to get up

se laver – to have a wash

s'habiller – to get dressed

se brosser les dents – to clean one's teeth

se coucher – to go to bed

se doucher – to take a shower

Key Point

- Lever is a regular verb, but it adds an accent in the present tense (apart from the *nous* and *vous* forms). Several other verbs add or change their accents in this way and it is important to learn them, so you can pronounce them correctly:
- préférer (to prefer) – je/on préfère, vous préférez, préféré
- acheter (to buy) – on/j'achète, vous achetez, acheté

Grammaire

You have already met several reflexive verbs in earlier sections, including *je m'appelle* (Section 1), *s'amuser* (Section 5) and *s'habiller, se maquiller* and *s'occuper de* (see page 72).

Reflexive verbs are formed in the same way as other verbs, but they add a pronoun between the subject and the verb. Reflexive verbs usually describe something you do to yourself, such as washing yourself or dressing yourself. Reflexive verbs are more common in French (we often translate them with 'get' in English). Take the verb *laver* (to wash), for example:

je lave la voiture – I wash the car

je **me** lave – I wash myself (I get washed/I have a wash)

The pronoun changes according to the subject of the verb:

se coucher – to go to bed

je **me** couche – I go to bed

tu **te** couches – you go to bed

il/elle/on **se** couche – he/she goes to bed

nous **nous** couchons – we go to bed

vous **vous** couchez – you go to bed

ils/elles **se** couchent – they go to bed

If the verb begins with a vowel, the reflexive pronoun is shortened:

je **m'**appelle   il **s'**appelle

The reflexive pronoun usually comes immediately before the verb in all tenses. In the perfect tense, it goes just before the auxiliary verb *être*:

je **me** suis amusé et je **me** suis couché à minuit – I had fun and went to bed at midnight

Écoutez et notez

Listen and select the correct verb.

1 Je me réveille/me lève à sept heures.

2 Il se couche/se brosse les dents à onze heures.

3 Elles s'occupent de/s'intéressent à leurs vêtements.

4 Je me lave/me brosse les cheveux.

5 On s'amuse/se lave bien.

6 Elle s'entend bien avec/s'occupe de sa sœur.

Key Point

Focus on learning the reflexive verbs you need to describe the most important parts of your daily routine. For example, if you take time with your hair every morning, learn: *je m'occupe de ma coiffure le matin*.

Progress Check

Tick all the possible translations of these verb phrases:

1 Je me suis bien amusé.

  a I amused Ben. ☐

  b I am amusing. ☐

  c I had fun. ☐

  d I amused myself. ☐

  e I have had a good time. ☐

2 Je me lave chaque jour.

  a I have a wash every day. ☐

  b I wash myself every day. ☐

  c Every day I get washed. ☐

  d I wash it every day. ☐

1 c, d, e, 2 a, b, c

6.5 Quand j'étais jeune ...

Écoutez et lisez

En France, en général, on ne porte pas d'uniforme à l'école. Autrefois, on portait des tabliers à l'école. C'était une sorte de chemise bleue ou rouge que l'on portait par dessus les autres vêtements. La première semaine tout le monde portait un tablier rouge et la deuxième semaine tout le monde portait un tablier bleu. Aujourd'hui, les français trouvent l'uniforme scolaire dans les écoles britanniques un peu bizarre. En France au collège on porte un jean, un tee-shirt et des baskets. C'est peut-être aussi un uniforme, non?

✎ Now underline all the present tense verbs.

Vocabulaire

l'uniforme scolaire
– school uniform

par dessus
– on top of

quand j'étais jeune
– when I was young

autrefois
– in the past, in the olden days

un tablier
– smock, pinafore, apron, overall

aujourd'hui
– today, nowadays

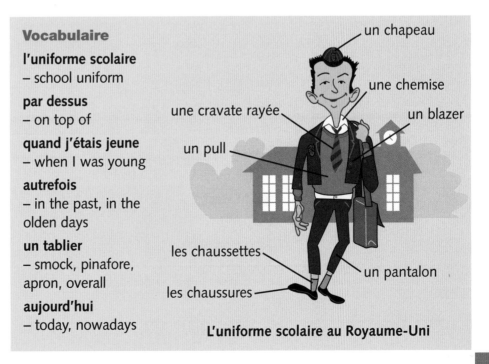

un chapeau
une chemise
une cravate rayée
un blazer
un pull
les chaussettes
les chaussures
un pantalon

L'uniforme scolaire au Royaume-Uni

Grammaire

If you want to talk about something in the past that happened frequently or lasted a long time, or if you want to describe something from the past, you use the imperfect tense. It is easy to learn the examples of imperfect tense verbs you are most likely to use:

avoir

j'avais – I had, I was having, I used to have

on avait – we/you had, we/you were having, we/you used to have

il y avait – there was/were, there used to be

être

j'étais – I was, I used to be

on était – we/you were, we/you used to be

c'était – it was, it used to be

The imperfect endings of -er verbs are easy to recognise:

porter – to give

je port**ais**	nous port**ions**
tu port**ais**	vous port**iez**
il/elle/on port**ait**	il/elles port**aient**

Lisez et trouvez les verbes

Read the text and find the imperfect tense verbs translated below.

Quand j'étais jeune, j'allais à l'école maternelle. Je portais un uniforme scolaire et j'adorais ça. On portait un sweat avec le nom de l'école et un pantalon gris. Le week-end mes vêtements préférés étaient un jean rose et un sweat jaune avec une image de Winnie l'Ourson. Ma mère les lavait chaque soir parce que je voulais les porter chaque jour, sans exception. Bof, j'avais des préférences bizarres!

1 I was (young) _____

2 I used to go _____

3 I used to wear _____

4 I loved it _____

5 we wore _____

6 (my favourite clothes) were _____

7 used to wash _____

8 I wanted to _____

9 I used to have _____

Progress Check

Which of the following are possible translations of the sentence:

Quand j'étais jeune, j'aimais les tortues Ninja et ma sœur avait une Barbie.

a When I was young I used to have some Ninja turtles and my sister used to like Barbie.

b When I was young I used to like Ninja turtles and my sister had a Barbie.

c When I was young I liked Ninja turtles and my sister used to have a Barbie.

d When I was young I had some Ninja turtles and my sister liked Barbie.

e When I was young I used to like Ninja turtles and my sister used to have a Barbie.

ə puɐ ɔ ʻq

Key Point

In exams, you might be expected to read a variety of different types of texts. This might include reading and understanding a simple poem.

J'aime lire!

Read the poem and insert the missing lines into the right places in the English translation over the page.

POLYCHROMIE

Cher frère blanc
Quand je suis né, j'étais noir,
Quand j'ai grandi, j'étais noir,
Quand je vais au soleil, je suis noir
Quand j'ai peur, je suis noir
Quand je suis malade, je suis noir …
Tandis que toi, homme blanc
Quand tu es né, tu étais rose,
Quand tu as grandi, tu étais blanc
Quand tu vas au soleil, tu es rouge,
Quand tu as froid, tu es bleu,
Quand tu as peur, tu es vert,
Quand tu es malade, tu es jaune,
Et après cela tu oses m'appeler 'Homme de couleur'

(Anonyme Africain)

continuez >>>

<<< continuez

Dear white brother,

When I grew up, I was black

When I am afraid, I am black

Whereas, you, white man

When you grew up, you were white,

When you are cold, you are blue,

When you are ill, you are yellow,

And after that, you dare to call me a 'man of colour'?
When you are frightened, you are green,
When I am ill, I am black
When I go out in the sun, I am black
When you go out in the sun, you are red,
When you were born, you were pink,
When I was born, I was black

Mon dossier

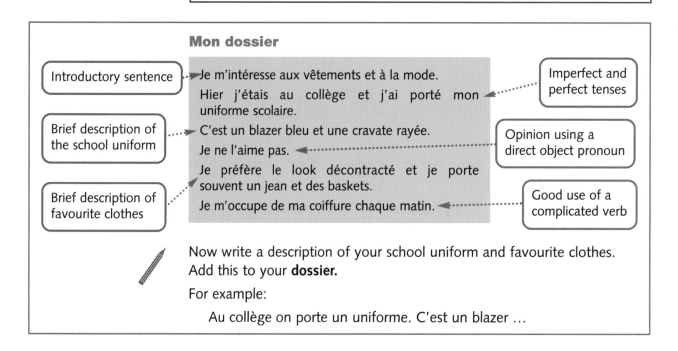

Introductory sentence → Je m'intéresse aux vêtements et à la mode.

Hier j'étais au collège et j'ai porté mon uniforme scolaire. ← Imperfect and perfect tenses

Brief description of the school uniform → C'est un blazer bleu et une cravate rayée.

Je ne l'aime pas. ← Opinion using a direct object pronoun

Brief description of favourite clothes → Je préfère le look décontracté et je porte souvent un jean et des baskets.

Je m'occupe de ma coiffure chaque matin. ← Good use of a complicated verb

Now write a description of your school uniform and favourite clothes. Add this to your **dossier**.

For example:

Au collège on porte un uniforme. C'est un blazer ...

Practice test questions

Listening 🎧 38

Listen to Sophie describing herself and her friends and write the name of the relevant person under each picture.

1 _____ 2 _____ 3 _____ 4 _____

| Sophie (moi) | Émilie | Mélissa | Tania |

(4 marks)

Speaking

Answer the questions in the role play in full sentences.

Bonjour, vous désirez?	Say you would like a leather jacket.
De quelle couleur?	Say you would like brown, please.
De quelle taille?	Say medium size.
Voilà une veste très chic. C'est trois cents euros.	Say that is too expensive and it doesn't suit you.
Voilà une veste plus décontractée. C'est cent euros.	Say you like it and that you'll take it.
Voilà, je vous en prie.	Say thank you and goodbye.

(6 marks)

Reading

Read this poem about Africa and insert the correct colour to complete the English translation. The first one has been done for you.

L'Afrique

L'Afrique est noire comme ma peau	Africa is **black** _____ like my skin
Elle est rouge comme la terre.	It is _____ like the earth.
Elle est blanche comme la lumière de midi.	It is _____ like the midday light.
Elle est bleue comme l'ombre du soir.	It is _____ like the evening shade.
Elle est jaune comme le grand fleuve.	It is _____ like the big river.
Elle est verte comme la feuille du palmier.	It is _____ like the palm leaf.
L'Afrique a toutes les couleurs de la vie.	Africa has all the colours of life.

(Marie Sellier)

(5 marks)

Writing

Write sentences describing this girl's routine in the morning.

Exemple:

__Elle se réveille à sept heures.__

4

_____

1

_____

5

_____

2

_____

6

_____

3

_____

7

_____

(7 marks)

After studying this topic you should be able to:

- talk about the weather now and in the past
- talk about the transport you use
- describe the area where you live and give your opinion of it
- understand texts about environmental problems and their solutions
- know more about the Paris metro

7.1 Quel temps fait-il?

Vocabulaire

Quel temps fait-il? – What's the weather like?

Il fait beau/mauvais – The weather's nice/bad (miserable)

Il fait froid/chaud – It's hot/cold

Il fait du soleil/du brouillard – It's sunny/foggy

Il fait du vent – It's windy

Il pleut – It's raining/it rains

Il neige – It's snowing/it snows

Pleuvoir, neiger and geler are impersonal verbs. This means that they do not refer to a **person** doing something and can only be used with *il*, e.g. **il** pleut – **it** is raining.

Key Point

All the weather phrases formed with *il fait du ...* can also be used with *il y a du ...* e.g. il fait du vent / il y a du vent – it is windy.

Écoutez et complétez le plan

France is a big country and the weather in the different parts can be very different on the same day, especially in winter. Listen to this weather forecast and fill in the weather map with the correct symbols, as shown in the vocabulaire box above. (To revise compass points, see page 15.)

You can replace 'quand' in these phrases with '**si**', e.g. s'il fait beau – if it's nice weather.

Grammaire

Quand (when) is usually used as a question word, but it can also be used as a link word to join two different ideas:

Quand il fait beau, je vais à la plage – When the weather is nice, I go to the beach

Quand il fait mauvais, je reste à la maison – When the weather is bad, I stay home

Quand je vais en ville, je fais les magasins – When I go to town, I go shopping

Quand je vais à une soirée, je mets mes vêtements chics – When I go to a party, I wear smart clothes

Quand je vais au collège, je porte mon uniforme scolaire – When I go to school, I wear my uniform

Progress Check

Complete these sentences, saying what you do in each kind of weather.

1 Quand il fait beau, …

2 Quand il fait mauvais, …

3 Quand il neige, …

4 Quand il pleut, …

5 Quand il fait chaud, …

Many answers are possible. See the *Grammaire* box above for examples.

7.2 Quel temps faisait-il hier?

Écoutez et lisez

Hier c'était une journée parfaite ici en France. Il y avait du soleil partout. Il faisait chaud au bord de la mer. À la montagne il faisait beau, mais pas aussi chaud. Il y avait un petit peu de brouillard le matin, mais il n'y avait pas de vent. Quelle journée formidable!

Quelle journée formidable! – What a wonderful day!

Vocabulaire

Quel temps faisait-il hier? – What was the weather like yesterday?

il faisait beau/froid/du brouillard – it was nice/cold/foggy

il y avait du vent/du soleil – it was windy/sunny

il y avait un orage – there was a storm

il neigeait/pleuvait – it was snowing/raining

partout – everywhere

Key Point

Use the imperfect tense to describe what the weather was like in the past. This is a good way to add more detail to an account of your last holiday, for example, and to improve your mark.

Regardez et complétez

Complete the sentences describing yesterday's weather according to the weather map.

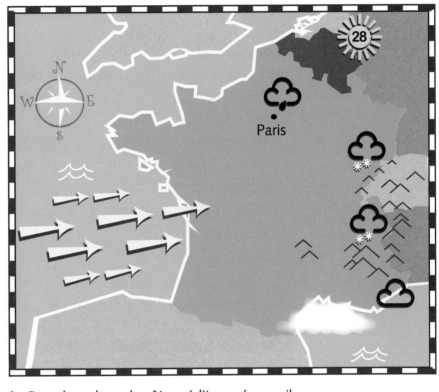

1 Dans le sud, sur la côte méditerranéenne, il _____

2 À la montagne, dans les Alpes, il _____

3 Dans l'ouest de la France, il _____

4 À Paris, il _____

5 Au nord-est de la France, il _____

Progress Check

Translate these sentences into English:

1 Hier il y avait du brouillard.

2 Il faisait mauvais hier.

3 Hier il pleuvait.

4 Il y avait un grand orage hier.

5 Hier il faisait du vent.

5 Yesterday it was windy.
4 There was a big storm yesterday.
3 Yesterday it was raining/rained.
2 The weather was bad/miserable yesterday.
1 Yesterday there was some fog.

7.3 Le transport

Écoutez et lisez

Pour aller au collège, normalement j'y vais à vélo. Mais hier il pleuvait et j'y suis allé en voiture avec ma mère. Quand je vais en ville, il vaut mieux utiliser les transports en commun et donc je prends le bus pour y aller. Le centre sportif n'est pas loin de chez moi. J'y vais à pied. L'année dernière je suis allé en Angleterre et j'ai pris le tunnel en Eurostar.

il vaut mieux
– it is better to

Vocabulaire

le transport en commun – public transport

le bus – bus

le train – train

le métro – underground train

l'avion (m) – aircraft

la voiture – car

l'Eurostar (m) – Eurostar

la gare – train station

la station – underground station

une correspondance – a station where you can change from one line to another

changer de train – to change trains

la ligne – train line

le RER – suburban train system in Paris (which covers a wider area than the *Métro*)

la moto – (small) motorbike

le vélo – bike

le cheval – horse

à pied – on foot

y – there

jusqu'à – as far as

donc – so

Grammaire

There are various ways to say 'to go' in French:

aller – to go
use with *en* + a form of transport (except for à *vélo* and à *pied*)
   je vais en voiture – I go by car

prendre – to take
use with a determiner + form of transport:
   pour aller en ville, je prends le métro – to go into town, I take the underground

partir – to leave
   l'avion part à quatre heures – the plane leaves at 4 o'clock

continuez >>>

<<< continuez

voyager – to travel

use to describe longer journeys or holidays

> je veux voyager à Venise en Orient-Express – I want to travel to Venice on the Orient Express

There are some phrases which use 'go' in English, but a different verb in French:

> faire du ski – to go skiing

> faire les magasins – to go shopping

> faire une promenade à vélo
> faire du vélo } to go for a bike ride

Être en train de faire is an expression meaning to be in the middle of doing something, e.g. – *on est en train de manger* – we are in the middle of eating at the moment, *je suis en train de faire mes examens* – I am in the middle of my exams.

All of France loves 'le Tour de France', the famous international cycle race which is now over 100 years old. It takes place annually in July and covers France and several neighbouring countries. The leader at each stage wears 'le maillot jaune' (the yellow jersey).

Grammaire

The pronoun *y* means 'there' and is used to avoid repeating the name of a place:

> Je vais **au collège** en bus.

> J'**y** vais en bus.

The pronoun usually comes immediately before the verb, but if there are two verbs, *y* comes before the second verb:

> J'aime la montagne. On peut **y** faire du ski.

Imaginez le voyage

Imagine you are travelling to Disneyland™ Resort Paris. Rearrange the sentences into the correct order to describe each stage of your journey. Use the sequencing adverbs *(d'abord, puis, finalement)* as clues.

a Arrivé à Paris, on prend le métro jusqu'à la station Châtelet les Halles. ☐

b D'abord, je pars de chez moi en voiture. **1**

c Et voilà, Disneyland! ☐

d Finalement on y prend le train RER jusqu'à la gare Marne-la-Vallée-Chessy. ☐

e Là il y a une correspondance sur la ligne RER A4. **7**

f On arrive à la Gare du Nord à Paris. ☐

g On change de train et on voyage en Eurostar sous la Manche. **4**

h On va à la gare en voiture. ☐

i Puis on prend le train jusqu'à la gare Waterloo à Londres. ☐

Progress Check

Complete each sentence with the correct preposition, *en* or *à*, the pronoun *y*, or a determiner.

1 Je prends _____ bus pour aller chez ma grand-mère.

2 Je vais _____ la gare _____ vélo.

3 L'année dernière, j'ai voyagé _____ train.

4 Je suis au collège en cinq minutes. J'_____ vais _____ pied.

5 Je vais en ville _____ voiture avec ma mère.

1 le, 2 à à, 3 en, 4 y à, 5 en

7.4 Ma région

Écoutez et lisez

J'habite à Sochaux. C'est une ville industrielle dans la région Franche-Comté à 440 kilomètres de Paris. C'est un peu sale. Dans ma ville il y a un centre commercial. Je n'aime pas beaucoup ma ville parce que c'est ennuyeux et trop loin de la mer.

La meilleure chose dans ma ville, c'est que les gens sont sympas.

La pire chose dans ma ville, c'est la pollution.

Now underline all the adjectives used to describe Sochaux.

Sochaux in the east of France is perhaps best known for its football team. Peugeot cars are manufactured here also. Most people in the town work for Peugeot and visitors can see the 'Musée Peugeot à Sochaux'. Unfortunately, the industry causes pollution in the area.

Vocabulaire

il y a beaucoup à faire – there is lots to do

les gens sont sympas – the people are nice

c'est (assez) près de la mer – it's (quite) close to the sea

il y a un (grand) centre commercial – there's a (big) shopping centre

il n'y a rien à faire – there's nothing to do

il n'y a pas de (piscine) – there is no (swimming pool)

c'est trop cher – it's too expensive

c'est sale/pollué – it's dirty/polluted

il y a trop de circulation – there's too much traffic

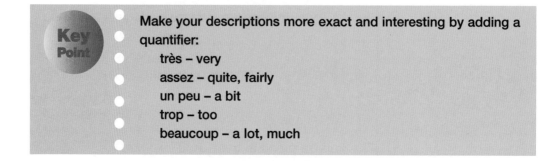

Key Point

Make your descriptions more exact and interesting by adding a quantifier:

  très – very

  assez – quite, fairly

  un peu – a bit

  trop – too

  beaucoup – a lot, much

The United Kingdom is one of the few places in the world that uses miles instead of kilometres. When you describe a distance in French, you need to be able to say it in kilometres. To convert miles roughly into kilometres, times it by 1.5. For example it's about 400 miles from London to Edinburgh, which is roughly 600 kilometres.

Décrivez votre région

Use the following writing frame to describe your home town or area. You can include vocabulary from section 5.2.

Where do you live?	J'habite à _____
Whereabouts is it?	C'est dans la région _____
How far is it from other places?	À _____ kilomètres de _____
What kind of place is it?	C'est _____
What is there in your town?	Dans ma ville il y a _____
Do you like your town? Why?	J'aime/Je n'aime pas ma ville, parce que _____
What is the best thing about your town?	La meilleure chose dans ma ville, c'est (que) _____
And what is the worst thing?	La pire chose dans ma ville, c'est _____

Grammaire

Qui and *que* are not only used as question words (see page 141) but can also be used as relative pronouns meaning 'who', 'which' or 'that'. Relative pronouns join parts of a sentence and can never be left out in French, unlike in English:

> un film, **que** j'aime – a film (that) I like

> le film **qui** a gagné l'Oscar – the film that won the Oscar

Qui or que?

If you can leave out the relative pronoun in the English sentence, that means you should use *que* in French. If you can't leave it out, use *qui*:

> un film **que** j'ai vu – a film (that) I have seen

> un acteur, **que** j'adore – an actor (whom) I love

> une actrice **qui** danse bien – an actress who dances well

Progress Check

Rearrange these sentences into the correct order.

1 a de Il magasins. n'y pas

2 sale. est C' très

3 a circulation. de Il trop y

4 a commercial centre Il moderne. un y

5 assez gens Les sympas. sont

1 Il n'y a pas de magasins.
2 C'est très sale.
3 Il y a trop de circulation.
4 Il y a un centre commercial moderne.
5 Les gens sont assez sympas.

7.5 L'environnement

The environment is a topic where you would usually be expected to understand the language rather than being able to use it yourself. Given much of the vocabulary is very similar to the English, this is not too difficult.

Vocabulaire

problèmes de l'environnement – environmental problems

la pollution – pollution

le réchauffement de la planète – global warming

la destruction des forêts – the destruction of forests

les déchets toxiques – toxic waste

l'exploitation des animaux – exploitation of animals

pour protéger l'environnement – to protect the environment

pour sauver la planète – to save the planet

il faut – we/you must, it's essential

on peut – we/you can

je dois – I must

recycler – to recycle

éviter l'accumulation des déchets – avoid waste

utiliser les transports en commun – use public transport

utiliser l'énergie solaire – use solar energy

respecter la planète – respect our planet

When you look up a verb in a French dictionary, you will usually find it in the infinitive form. The infinitive is the 'neutral' form of the verb. In English, it begins with 'to'. In French, infinitives are divided into three groups: -er verbs, -ir verbs and -re verbs.

Grammaire

There are several phrases which are very useful, as all you need to do is add an infinitive:

> pour (+ infinitive) – in order to …

je peux – I can
on peut – we/you/they can
je dois – I must

il vaut mieux de – it is better to
il faut – we/you must, it's essential

Écoutez et notez

Listen to the recording and note the order in which the environmental problems and solutions are discussed:

Pour sauver la planète il faut arrêter la destruction des forêts. ☐

Il faut respecter la planète. ☐

On peut utiliser l'énergie solaire pour éviter le réchauffement de la planète. ☐

Pour éviter la pollution on peut utiliser les transports en commun. ☐

Pour éviter l'accumulation des déchets je dois recycler. ☐

Progress Check

Translate the vocabulary into English.

1 les transports en commun

2 l'exploitation des animaux

3 le réchauffement de la planète

4 la destruction des forêts

5 protéger la planète

5 protect the planet
4 the destruction of forests
3 global warming
2 exploitation of animals
1 public transport

J'aime lire!

Le *métropolitain* parisien a 199 kilomètres de longueur. Il y a 368 stations, c'est presque une centaine de stations de plus que l'Underground à Londres. On l'appelle affectueusement *le métro*. La première ligne de métro – bien sûr la ligne 1 – était ouverte en 1900. C'était l'époque du mouvement Art Nouveau et donc on a créé des entrées de stations originales dans ce style.

La ligne 4 était la première ligne du métro à traverser la Seine en 1906. En 1963, pour la première fois un métro roule sur des pneus pour un voyage plus confortable. Le métro n'était pas le premier chemin de fer souterrain dans le monde, mais maintenant on utilise le mot 'métro' partout pour parler des trains souterrains.

To say **in** a year, use *en*: Je suis né *en* 1996. – I was born **in** 1996.

le pneu – (rubber) tyre

le chemin de fer – railway

souterrain – underground, subterranean

Key Point

Scanning a text for numbers is a good way of getting a rough idea of what the text is about. Search for the numbers then work out what each number refers to.

Répondez aux questions en anglais

1 When did the first line of the Paris metro open?
_____

2 Which underground network has more stations, Paris or London?
_____

3 Which metro line opened in 1900?
_____

4 Why are some station entrances and signs in the Art Nouveau style?
_____

5 Which line was the first one to cross the river Seine?
_____

6 Why were rubber tyres added to the train cars in 1963?
_____

7 Is the Paris metro the oldest underground railway in the world?
_____

8 What is special about the word *métro* or metro?
_____

Mon dossier

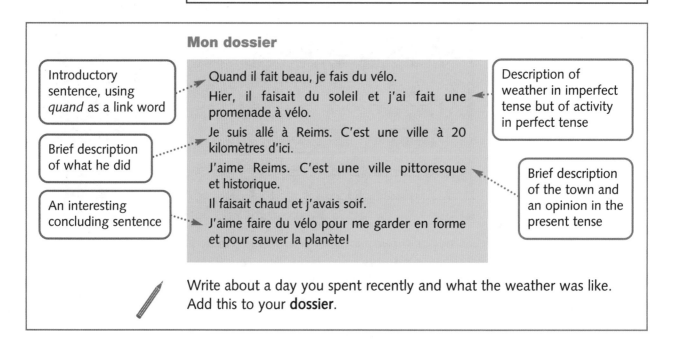

Introductory sentence, using *quand* as a link word

Brief description of what he did

An interesting concluding sentence

Quand il fait beau, je fais du vélo.
Hier, il faisait du soleil et j'ai fait une promenade à vélo.
Je suis allé à Reims. C'est une ville à 20 kilomètres d'ici.
J'aime Reims. C'est une ville pittoresque et historique.
Il faisait chaud et j'avais soif.
J'aime faire du vélo pour me garder en forme et pour sauver la planète!

Description of weather in imperfect tense but of activity in perfect tense

Brief description of the town and an opinion in the present tense

Write about a day you spent recently and what the weather was like. Add this to your **dossier**.

Practice test questions

Listening 🎧 **44**

Listen to the weather forecast and draw the weather symbols in the correct places on the map.

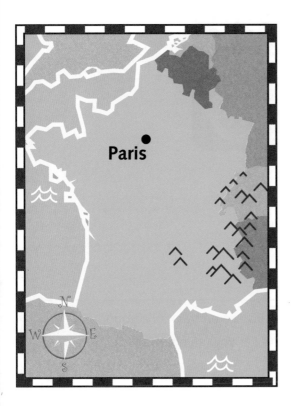

(4 marks)

Speaking

Say what you do in different types of weather. The first one has been done for you.

Exemple:    Quand il fait beau, je travaille dans le jardin.

1

2

3

4

5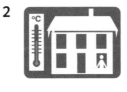

(5 marks)

Reading

Match the correct sentence to each picture to describe this journey.

L'année dernière je suis allé en France.

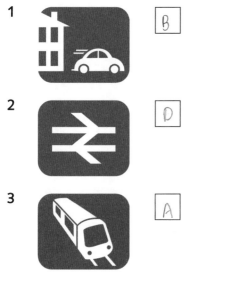

1 B

2 D

3 A

4 E

5 C

C'était un voyage long!

a Je suis arrivé à la gare.	**d** Je suis allé en train à l'aéroport.
b Je suis parti de chez moi en voiture.	**e** Puis j'ai voyagé en avion.
c Finalement, j'ai pris le métro.	

(5 marks)

Writing

Match up the correct halves of these sentences about Carcassonne.
The first one has been done for you.

J'habite à ___*Carcassonne.*_____

C'est dans _____

C'est à cent _____

C'est pittoresque et _____

Dans ma ville il y a _____

J'aime ma ville, parce que _____

La pire chose dans ma ville, c'est _____

~~Carcassonne.~~	kilomètres de Toulouse.	qu'il y a trop de touristes.
c'est intéressant.	la région Languedoc-Roussillon.	un grand château et la vieille ville.
historique.		

(6 marks)

La santé

After studying this topic you should be able to:

- name the parts of the body
- describe what's wrong with you
- use adjectives correctly
- understand advice given on health issues
- talk about health, fitness and a healthy diet

Écoutez et lisez

Ça va?

Non, pas du tout.

Qu'est-ce que tu as?

Je ne sais pas, mais j'ai mal à la gorge et j'ai mal au dos. J'ai aussi mal à la tête.

Tu as mal à l'estomac? Tu as faim?

Non, je n'ai pas mangé.

Tu as chaud?

Oui, j'ai très chaud et j'ai soif aussi.

Peut-être que tu as la grippe.

Alors, qu'est-ce qu'il faut faire?

Reste au lit et bois beaucoup d'eau.

D'accord.

Je ne sais pas =
I don't know

✏ Underline all the parts of avoir in the dialogue.
How many of each different form are there?

8.1 Le corps

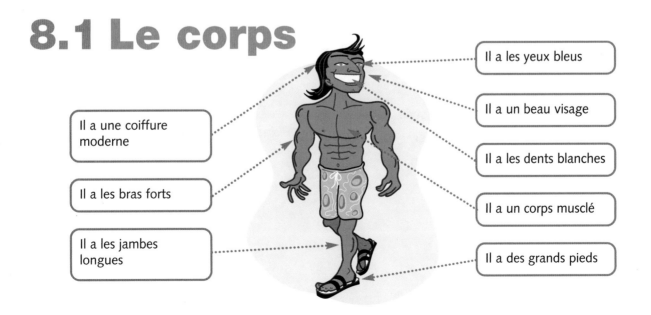

Il a les yeux bleus

Il a un beau visage

Il a les dents blanches

Il a un corps musclé

Il a une coiffure moderne

Il a les bras forts

Il a les jambes longues

Il a des grands pieds

Cherchez dans le dictionnaire

Use your dictionary to find the French plurals and English translation for these parts of the body:

la bouche   _____   _____

le corps   _____   _____

le cou   _____   _____

la dent   _____   _____

le doigt   _____   _____

le dos   _____   _____

le genou   _____   _____

la gorge   _____   _____

le nez   _____   _____

See page 13 for more on adjectives and their agreements.

Grammaire

In French, adjectives usually go *after* the nouns they're describing. There are a few, however, that go *before* the noun.

Il a un **beau** visage – He has a beautiful face

Il a des **grands** pieds – He has big feet

Learn them in pairs. Many of the adjectives are irregular, so you need to learn the feminine forms, too:

grand(e)/petit(e) – big/small

jeune/vieux(vieille) – young/old

bon(ne)/mauvais(e) – good/bad

nouveau(nouvelle)/ancien(ne) – new/former

premier(première)/dernier(dernière) – first/last

beau(belle)/joli(e) – nice/pretty

Progress Check

Translate the following phrases into French, paying attention to the correct position and agreement of the adjective:

1 a big nose

2 a small child

3 a new hairstyle

4 bad weather

5 a young man

5 un jeune homme
4 un mauvais temps
3 une nouvelle coiffure
2 un petit enfant
1 un grand nez

8.2 Qu'est-ce que tu as?

To say 'Get better soon' to someone who is ill, say: **Bon rétablissement**.

To say a particular part of your body hurts, use *J'ai mal à ...* with a noun.

The form of the word *à* will vary, however, depending on the noun that follows it. (You have seen similar patterns on pages 51 and 118.) It doesn't change at all with feminine nouns:

> **la** main – hand
> J'ai mal **à la** main – my hand hurts

It does change, however, for masculine and plural nouns:

> **le** pied – foot
> J'ai mal **au** pied
>
> **les** mains – hands
> J'ai mal **aux** mains – my hands hurt
>
> **les** pieds – feet
> J'ai mal **aux** pieds

Some nouns follow a slightly different pattern:

> J'ai mal à **l'**oreille – my ear hurts (one ear)
> J'ai mal **aux** oreilles – my ears hurt (two ears)
>
> J'ai mal à **l'**œil – my eye hurts (one eye)
> J'ai mal **aux** yeux – my eyes hurt (both eyes)

You should also be able to describe general things that are wrong with you, as well as more specific problems with particular parts of the body.

Vocabulaire

Qu'est-ce qu tu as? – What is wrong with you?

J'ai chaud – I am hot

J'ai froid – I am cold

J'ai faim – I am hungry

J'ai la grippe – I have flu

J'ai peur – I am scared

J'ai soif – I am thirsty

J'ai sommeil – I am sleepy

J'ai envie de ... – I want to ...

J'ai besoin de ... – I need ...

Avoir

Revise the verb avoir on page 38.

In French you sometimes use the verb *avoir* where we might say 'I am' in English:

> **J'ai** treize ans – I am thirteen (years old)

But some important phrases use *être* as we do in English:

> Je suis malade – I am ill   Je suis fatigué(e) – I am tired

Use the right part of *avoir* to describe someone else's problems:

> Elle a mal à la tête – she has a headache
>
> Nous avons mal à la gorge – we have sore throats

Écoutez et notez

Listen to the conversations and note in English what is wrong with each person.

1 _____
_____

2 _____
_____

3 _____
_____

4 _____
_____

Progress Check

To say you have a cold in French, you can say *Je suis enrhumé(e)*. How many possible symptoms of a cold can you name?

Possible answers:
j'ai mal à la tête/gorge
j'ai mal au dos/nez
j'ai mal aux oreilles
j'ai chaud/froid/sommeil
je suis malade/fatigué(e)

8.3 Qu'est-ce qu'il faut faire?

People give you lots of advice when you're ill!

Vocabulaire

Qu'est-ce qu'il faut faire? – What should I do?

restez au lit – stay in bed

prenez cette ordonnance – take this prescription

allez à l'hôpital – go to the hospital

buvez beaucoup d'eau – drink lots of water

mangez du yaourt – eat some yogurt

évitez le soleil – avoid the sun

utilisez un sparadrap – use a plaster

All these pieces of advice are given in the imperative form, which you met on pages 9 and 10. Remember that the *vous* form would be used to address an adult or group of people and the *tu* form would be used to a child or someone you know well.

Devinez et écoutez

Katie is on holiday in the south of France and stayed too long in the sun yesterday. Read the list of *Conseils* (advice) that she might get at a chemist's. Tick the ones you think are the best advice for mild sunstroke (*un coup de soleil*) in the blue column. Then listen to the conversation between Katie and the pharmacist and check to see if your predictions were correct.

Conseils	Mes prédictions	✗ ou ✔?
1 Allez chez le dentiste	✗	✗
2 Allez à la piscine		
3 Prenez des aspirines		
4 Utilisez un sparadrap		
5 Ne mangez pas		
6 Mangez des légumes		
7 Évitez les chiens		
8 Évitez le soleil		
9 Buvez beaucoup d'eau		
10 Utilisez une crème		
11 Restez à la maison		
12 Restez au lit		

Progress Check

Match the advice with the problem:

1 Je suis très malade.
2 J'ai mal aux dents.
3 J'ai mal à l'estomac.
4 J'ai soif.
5 J'ai sommeil.

a Restez au lit.
b Allez à l'hôpital.
c Buvez beaucoup d'eau.
d Mangez du yaourt.
e Allez chez le dentiste.

1b, 2e, 3d, 4c, 5a

8.4 Tu es en forme?

Écoutez et lisez

Qu'est-ce que tu fais pour être en forme?

Pour être en forme, je fais du sport assez souvent. J'ai toujours aimé la natation et deux fois par semaine je vais à la piscine. Je mange très sainement et je mange des fruits et des légumes quatre ou cinq fois par jour. Normalement j'évite le coca. Quelquefois je mange dans un fast-food avec mes amis. Je refuse toujours les cigarettes parce que c'est bête et le tabac est très dangereux. D'habitude je me couche assez tôt, mais le week-end je me couche plus tard. Je veux éviter le stress mais j'ai trop de devoirs chaque jour.

continuez >>>

<<< continuez

 What does the speaker do:

quite often? (assez souvent)	_____
twice a week? (deux fois par semaine)	_____
four or five times a day? (quatre ou cinq fois par jour)	_____
usually? (normalement)	_____
sometimes? (quelquefois)	_____
always? (toujours)	_____
at weekends? (le week-end)	_____
every day? (chaque jour)	_____

Key Point

Use frequency expressions, such as 'often', 'rarely', 'always', etc., to improve your speaking and writing, and to improve your grade.

Je fais du vélo – I ride my bike

Normalement, je fais du vélo **chaque jour** – Usually I ride my bike **every day**

Vocabulaire

une vie saine – a healthy life

pour être en forme – to keep fit

se garder **en forme** – to look after your health

se coucher **tôt/tard** – to go to bed early/late

boire de l'eau/du coca – to drink water/cola

manger du chocolat/des fruits/des légumes – to eat chocolate/fruit/vegetables

fumer – to smoke

refuser les cigarettes – to refuse cigarettes

aller au collège à pied/à vélo/en voiture – to go to school on foot/by bike/by car

faire du sport – to do sport

éviter le stress – to avoid stress

Se garder and se coucher are reflexive verbs. Look at page 80 to remind yourself how these are used.

Complétez les phrases

How often do you do each of the following? Choose a frequency expression from the Venn diagram below to complete each sentence. Look carefully at the diagram to put the frequency expression into the correct position, either before or after the verb phrase.

1 _____ je fais de la natation _____

2 _____ je mange du chocolat _____

3 _____ je bois un coca _____

4 _____ je vais au collège en voiture _____

5 _____ je me couche tôt _____

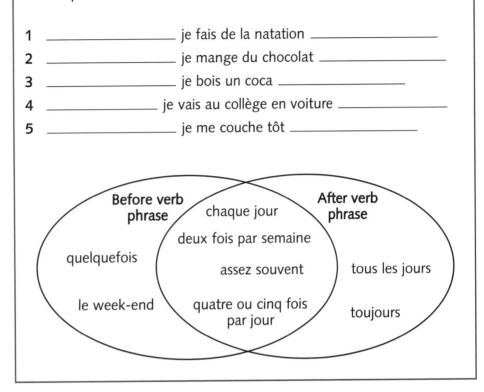

Before verb phrase

After verb phrase

chaque jour

deux fois par semaine

assez souvent

quelquefois

le week-end

quatre ou cinq fois par jour

tous les jours

toujours

Lisez et répondez

Read the quiz and work out which answers you would select if, first, you look after your health perfectly, and, second, you are a walking health disaster.

Jeu-test: Es-tu en forme?

		a	b	c
1	Je fais du sport	a chaque jour.	b une fois par mois.	c une fois par semaine.
2	Je mange les fast-foods	a trois fois par jour.	b pas souvent.	c quelquefois.
3	Je bois le plus souvent	a du coca.	b un jus de fruits.	c de l'eau minérale.
4	Je trouve que les légumes verts sont	a beurk!	b assez bons.	c ma nourriture préférée.
5	Je me couche	a tôt.	b quand je veux.	c toujours trop tard.

Healthy person's answers: 1 ☐ 2 ☐ 3 ☐ 4 ☐ 5 ☐

Unhealthy person's answers: 1 ☐ 2 ☐ 3 ☐ 4 ☐ 5 ☐

8.5 Des bonnes résolutions

Des bonnes
résolutions –
resolutions, good
intentions. Note how
the adjective goes
before the noun.

Nobody is perfect, so we could all do a bit more to look after our health. You can use the infinitives in the Key Vocabulary on page 104 with the following structures to talk about what you have to do and what you intend to do to improve your health:

je vais
je dois
il faut
on peut
il vaut mieux
} manger plus de légumes

Sometimes improving your health requires you to say what you will NOT do. You met various different negative expressions on page 41. The indefinite articles *un*, *une* and *des* change to *de* after a negative:

je mange **des** légumes – je ne mange jamais **de** légumes

je veux **un** coca – je ne veux pas **de** coca

il y a **du** chocolat – il n'y a pas **de** chocolat

Key Point

Talking about your health is a topic where you are likely to use several different tenses:

present tense – to say what you do for your health now
Le week-end je fais du sport.

past tense – to say what you have been doing or used to do to keep fit
La semaine dernière j'ai fait du sport.

future tense – to state your resolutions for looking after your health
Après les examens je vais faire plus de sport.

De is also used after *trop* and *beaucoup* when you are talking about quantities of things:

Il y a beaucoup de devoirs – There is a lot of homework

J'ai mangé trop de chocolat – I have eaten too much chocolate

De is shortened to *d'* before a vowel:

Il n'y a pas **d'**oranges – There aren't any oranges

Trouvez la traduction

Find the correct translation for each of these sentences.

1 Je ne veux pas de fruits.
2 Je n'ai pas acheté de fruits.
3 Il n'y a pas de fruits.
4 Je ne mange jamais de fruits.
5 Il n'y a plus de fruits.
6 J'ai mangé trop de fruits.
7 Il y a beaucoup de fruits.

a There isn't any fruit.
b I never eat fruit.
c I don't want (any) fruit.
d There is no more fruit.
e I haven't bought (any) fruit.
f There is a lot of fruit.
g I have eaten too much fruit.

Progress Check

Do these sentences describe a healthy lifestyle? Answer 'oui' or 'non' for each.

1 Je ne mange trop de chocolat.
2 Je vais au lit très tard.
3 Je mange des fruits chaque jour.
4 Le sport, c'est toujours dangereux.
5 Je vais au collège en voiture.

1 Oui
2 Non
3 Oui
4 Non
5 Non

J'aime lire!

Un sondage au sujet du tabac

Tout le monde sait que le tabac est dangereux. Mais selon un sondage récent, trente pour cent des jeunes fument. Les résultats du sondage sont affreux: la majorité des fumeurs ont commencé à fumer avant l'âge de dix-huit ans. La plupart des jeunes trouvent la pub pour le tabac amusante ou intéressante. Aujourd'hui, il y a plus de filles que de garçons qui fument.

Pourquoi est-ce que ces jeunes fumeurs veulent gaspiller leur argent pour cette dépendance? Les trois quarts fument, pour faire comme les autres. Quelques-uns pensent que c'est cool. Mais sept fumeurs sur dix veulent arrêter. Et un fumeur sur deux va mourir à cause de cette mauvaise habitude. Et ça doit être cool?

Match each quantity phrase with the correct item from the box below.

1 Thirty per cent
2 The majority of smokers
3 The majority of young smokers
4 Three-quarters
5 Some
6 Seven out of ten smokers
7 One smoker in two

a find tobacco advertising funny or interesting.
b of young people smoke.
c smoke to be like others.
d started to smoke before the age of 18.
e think it's cool.
f will die from this habit.
g want to give up.

Vocabulaire

You can use these phrases to write up the results of any survey.

les résultats sont … – the results are …

la plupart des gens – the majority of people   **aiment** – like

la majorité – the majority   **ont** – have

quelques-un – some people   **regardent** – watch

huit sur dix – eight out of ten   **sont** – are

vont – are going to   **veulent** – want

Mon dossier

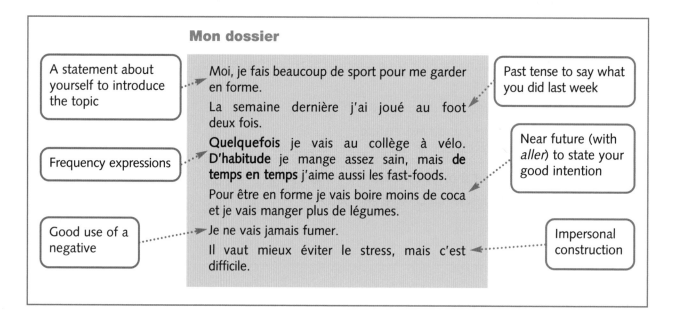

A statement about yourself to introduce the topic

Frequency expressions

Good use of a negative

Moi, je fais beaucoup de sport pour me garder en forme.

La semaine dernière j'ai joué au foot deux fois.

Quelquefois je vais au collège à vélo. **D'habitude** je mange assez sain, mais **de temps en temps** j'aime aussi les fast-foods.

Pour être en forme je vais boire moins de coca et je vais manger plus de légumes.

Je ne vais jamais fumer.

Il vaut mieux éviter le stress, mais c'est difficile.

Past tense to say what you did last week

Near future (with *aller*) to state your good intention

Impersonal construction

Practice test questions

Listening 🎧 49

Listen to these people asking the pharmacist for advice. Note in English the problem and the advice given.

	Problem	Advice
Exemple	*Sunstroke*	*Avoid the sun for three days and stay at home.*
1	_____	_____
2	_____	_____
3	_____	_____
4	_____	_____
5	_____	_____
6	_____	_____
7	_____	_____
8	_____	_____
9	_____	_____
10	_____	_____

(20 marks)

Speaking

Answer the questions in the role play in full sentences.

Bonjour. Qu'est-ce que tu as?
(Say you have a headache.)

Tu as chaud?
(Say you are thirsty.)

Tu étais au soleil hier?
(Say you went to the beach.)

Tu as un coup de soleil.
(Ask what you need to do.)

Reste à la maison et bois beaucoup d'eau.
(Say thank you and goodbye.)

(5 marks)

Reading

Read what these people say about their lifestyles and decide whether what they say is healthy (✔) or not healthy (✗).

For example: Je fais de la natation une fois par semaine.　　　✔

1　Quand je vais à la plage j'évite d'aller au soleil.　　　_____

2　Je bois du coca chaque jour.　　　_____

3　Je bois de l'eau minérale quatre ou cinq fois par jour.　　　_____

4　Je mange dans des fast-foods trois fois par semaine.　　　_____

5　Je fume le week-end.　　　_____

6　Je fais souvent du sport.　　　_____

7　Je ne mange jamais de légumes verts.　　　_____

8　Je me couche tard.　　　_____

9　J'aime bien le jus de fruits.　　　_____

10　Je pense que le tabac est nul.　　　_____　　　**(10 marks)**

Writing

Write out your good intentions for getting or staying healthy in full sentences. The first one has been done for you.

Example: eat chocolate occasionally　　Je vais manger du chocolat de temps en temps.

1　do more sport　　_____

_____

2　refuse cigarettes　　_____

_____

3　go to bed early　　_____

_____

4　eat fruit every day　　_____

_____

5　avoid stress　　_____

_____

6　walk to school　　_____

_____

7　drink less cola　　_____

_____

8　eat more vegetables　　_____

_____

9　go into town by bike　　_____

_____

10　go swimming twice a week　　_____

_____

(10 marks)

After studying this topic you should be able to:

● use numbers and prices in French
● buy different quantities of food in a shop
● buy train and bus tickets
● ask for and give directions
● buy stamps at a post office
● know more about famous landmarks in Paris

9.1 À la charcuterie

Écoutez et lisez

Bonjour. Vous désirez?

Avez-vous du jambon, s'il vous plaît?

Bien sûr. Combien vous en voulez?

Alors, je voudrais quatre tranches de jambon.

C'est tout?

Non, c'est combien le pâté?

Dix-sept euros le kilo.

J'en prends cinq cents grammes.

Voilà. Encore quelque chose?

Oui. Qu'est-ce que vous avez comme plats préparés?

Nous avons des quiches et de la salade.

J'en veux un assortiment, s'il vous plaît. Et c'est tout.

Ça fait quarante-deux euros, s'il vous plaît.

✎ Underline all the numbers in the text.

Vocabulaire

la charcuterie – delicatessen

Vous désirez? – What would you like?

Combien vous en voulez? – How much of it would you like?

je voudrais – I would like

C'est tout? – Is that all?

C'est combien? – How much is that?

J'en prends cinq cents grammes. – I'll take 500 grams of that.

continuez >>>

<<< continuez

Encore quelque chose? – Anything else?

Qu'est-ce que vous avez comme …? – What kinds of … do you have?

plats préparés – ready-made dishes

J'en veux un assortiment – I'd like a selection

Ça fait … – That makes …

Donnez-moi … – Give me …

Il me faut … – I need …

Vocabulaire

1	un	23	vingt-trois, etc.
2	deux	30	trente
3	trois	40	quarante
4	quatre	50	cinquante
5	cinq	60	soixante
6	six	70	soixante-dix
7	sept	71	soixante et onze
8	huit	72	soixante-douze
9	neuf	73	soixante-treize, etc.
10	dix	80	quatre-vingts
11	onze	81	quatre-vingt-un
12	douze	82	quatre-vingt-deux, etc.
13	treize	90	quatre-vingt-dix
14	quatorze	91	quatre-vingt-onze
15	quinze	92	quatre-vingt-douze, etc.
16	seize	100	cent
17	dix-sept	101	cent un
18	dix-huit	200	deux cents
19	dix-neuf	201	deux cent un
20	vingt	1000	mille
21	vingt et un	2000	deux mille
22	vingt-deux	1 000 000	un million

Most countries in Europe, including France and Belgium, use euros and cents. You would usually see prices written like this: €3,50 (trois euros cinquante).

If you go food shopping in a small town in France, you are likely to buy food in small, specialist shops or at a farmers' market rather than at a supermarket. This means you have to be able to ask for the quantities you want:

une boîte de – a tin of

une bouteille de – a bottle of

cent grammes de – one hundred grams of

un kilo de – a kilo of

un litre de – a litre of

un morceau de – a piece of

un paquet de – a packet of

une portion de – a helping of

un pot de – a pot of

une/deux tranche(s) de – a slice of/two slices of

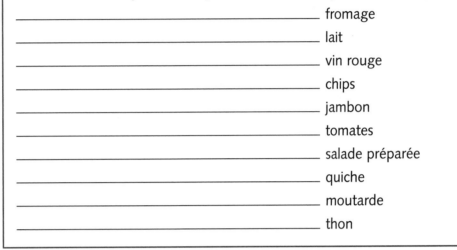

C'est quelle quantité?

Choose a suitable quantity for buying the following foods. (Look up the foods in a dictionary if necessary.) There are several possible answers.

_____ fromage

_____ lait

_____ vin rouge

_____ chips

_____ jambon

_____ tomates

_____ salade préparée

_____ quiche

_____ moutarde

_____ thon

Grammaire

Instead of asking for an exact quantity of food, you could just ask for 'some', using a partitive, which means the correct form of *de*. This is the same as the pattern you met on page 50.

Use *du* with masculine singular nouns:

du jambon, du pain, du vin

Use *de la* with feminine singular nouns:

de la salade, de la viande, de la confiture

Use *de l'* before a vowel:

de l'eau minérale

Use *des* before a plural noun:

des carottes, des croissants, des glaces

Expressions of quantity (e.g. 'a slice of') are always followed by *de*:

un pot de yaourt

Remember that *de* (or *d'*) is used after a negative (see page 106):

Nous n'avons pas de bananes

Grammaire

You have already met *en* used with years (page 95) and as a preposition of place (page 39). In the *Écoutez et lisez* text at the start of this section, you also saw how it can be used as a pronoun to replace nouns meaning 'some of that':

Combien vous **en** voulez? – How much of that do you want?

J'**en** prends cinq cents grammes – I'll take 500 grams of that

J'**en** veux un assortiment – I want a selection of that

The French for window-shopping – *faire du lèche-vitrines* – literally means 'licking shop windows'!

Vocabulaire

There are different expressions in French to describe the various kinds of shopping:

faire des achats – to go (food) shopping

faire les courses – to go shopping, to run errands

faire les magasins/les boutiques – to go (clothes) shopping

faire du shopping – to go shopping (for fun)

faire du lèche-vitrines – to go window-shopping

Progress Check

Translate the following sentences into English:

1 Je voudrais deux portions de quiche.

2 Tu as un paquet de chips?

3 C'est combien?

4 J'en veux deux mille.

5 Non, merci. C'est tout.

1 I would like two helpings of quiche.
2 Do you have a packet of crisps?
3 How much is that?
4 I want two thousand of them.
5 No, thanks. That's all.

9.2 Au café

Écoutez et lisez

51

Jérémy – Monsieur, la carte s'il vous plaît.

Le serveur – Voilà, Messieurs, Dames. Qu'est-ce que vous voulez boire?

Karima – Une grande bouteille d'eau minérale, et des cafés après.

Le serveur – Vous prenez le menu fixe ou vous mangez à la carte?

Élodie – Qu'est-ce que vous avez comme plat principal pour les végétariens?

Karima – Je suis musulmane, donc je ne mange pas de porc.

Jérémy – Et moi, je suis allergique au **blé**.

Élodie – Qu'est-ce que vous recommandez?

Le serveur – Je recommande le plat du jour, mais au restaurant à côté!

blé = wheat

Can you explain the joke? (See Vocabulaire on the next page for help.)

Instead of *manger* or *boire*, use *prendre*. It sounds more French.

Je mange un sandwich → Je prends un sandwich

Je bois un thé → Je prends un thé

Vocabulaire

la carte/le menu fixe – the menu/the fixed-price menu

Messieurs, Dames – Ladies and Gentlemen

manger à la carte – to select from the menu

Qu'est-ce que vous recommandez? – What do you recommend?

le plat principal/du jour – the main course/dish of the day

l'hors d'œuvre (m) – starter

le dessert – dessert

juif (juive) – Jewish

cacahouètes – peanuts

musulman(e) – Muslim

Écrivez des phrases

How would you explain to the waiter if you were ordering food on behalf of the following people? Use the table below to write sentences.

1   Your brother doesn't eat meat, because he's vegetarian.

2   Your girlfriend is a diabetic and eats no sugar.

3   Your father is allergic to wheat.

4   Your whole family is Jewish and eats no pork.

5   You don't eat peanuts.

Je Il Elle On	ne mange pas de	porc viande sucre fruits de mer blé fromage cacahouètes	parce que je suis parce qu'il est parce qu'elle est parce qu'on est	musulman(e) végétarien(ne) diabétique juif(juive) allergique

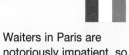

Waiters in Paris are notoriously impatient, so you have to be able to order quickly! The French word for waiter is *serveur*, but if you are speaking **to** a waiter, make sure you call him *Monsieur!*

Recopiez les plats dans la carte

Copy the names of the dishes from the box over the page into the correct section of the menu. Use a dictionary, if necessary.

Hors d'œuvres

Casse-croûtes

Plats principaux

Boissons

Desserts

continuez >>>

<<< continuez

Bifteck	Mélange de glaces
Côtelette d'agneau	Mousse au chocolat
Carafe de rouge	Omelette au choix
Citron pressé	Poisson du jour
Compote de fruits	Rôti de porc
Crêpe au fromage	Sandwich au pâté
Croque-monsieur	Salade de tomates
Crudités	Soupe du jour
Eau	Tarte aux pommes
Jus de fruit	

Key Point

Look up in a dictionary how to say your favourite and most hated foods, so you can describe your food preferences and any reasons for these preferences.

Progress Check

Find the appropriate answer to these questions asked in a restaurant:

1 Qu'est-ce que vous recommandez comme hors d'œuvre?
2 Est-ce qu'il y a un menu fixe?
3 Qu'est-ce que vous recommandez pour les végétariens?
4 Qu'est-ce que vous avez comme dessert?
5 Ça fait combien?

a L'omelette au fromage.
b Une crème caramel.
c Vingt-huits euros quarante-cinq.
d La soupe du jour.
e Je regrette, non. Vous pouvez manger à la carte.

1 d, 2 e, 3 a, 4 b, 5 c

9.3 En route

If you are travelling around a French-speaking country, you might need to buy travel tickets at some point. The language to buy all tickets is similar regardless of whether you are travelling by train, bus or metro.

France is justifiably proud of its fast and efficient train system, run by the SNCF (Société Nationale des Chemins de Fer). The TGV (*train à grande vitesse*) holds the world speed record for a train at 320.3mph (515.3 km/h). If it's carrying passengers, however, it usually goes no faster than 186 mph!

Vocabulaire

en route – on the way/let's go

un aller-retour – a return ticket

un aller simple – a single ticket

un billet pour … – a ticket for …

en première/deuxième classe – in first/second class

non-fumeurs – non-smoking

À quelle heure part le train pour …? – What time does the train for … leave?

De quel quai? – From which platform?

Il faut changer (de train)? – Do I have to change (trains)?

C'est quelle ligne/station pour …? – Which line/station is it for …?

Il y a une correspondance à … – There is an interchange at …

le prochain train/bus – the next train/bus

Ordinal numbers can be abbreviated, just as they are in English, for example: second ➞ 2nd. There are two ways to do this in French: deuxième ➞ 2e or 2ème

Vingt et unième ➞ 21e or 21ème

Grammaire

Ordinal numbers show the order of things, e.g. first, second, etc. There are two words for 'first' in French: *premier* (masculine) and *première* (feminine). Other ordinal numbers are usually formed by adding *-ième* to the end of the number.

Number	Ordinal
deux	deuxième
trois	troisième
vingt et un	vingt et unième
cent	centième

Écoutez et notez

52

Listen to these people buying tickets and write down what they ask for.

	Where to?	Ticket?
1		
2		
3		
4		
5		
6		

Progress Check

Translate these questions into English:

1 C'est quelle ligne pour la Gare du Nord, s'il vous plaît?

2 Est-ce qu'il faut changer de train?

3 C'est quelle station pour la Tour Eiffel, s'il vous plaît?

4 À quelle heure part le train pour Marseille?

5 C'est quand le prochain bus pour le centre-ville?

1 Which line is it for the Gare du Nord, please?
2 Do I have to change trains?
3 Which station is it for the Eiffel Tower, please?
4 What time does the train for Marseilles leave?
5 When is the next bus into town?

9.4 Pour aller à ...?

There are lots of different ways to ask how to get to a place, and lots of different answers too!

Vocabulaire

Pour aller à ...? – How do I get to ...?/What's the way to ...?

Où est/sont ...? – Where is/are ...?

Est-ce qu'il y a un/une ... près d'ici? – Is there a ... near here?

C'est loin? – Is it far?

C'est à 100 mètres – It's 100 metres away

allez/tournez à droite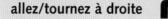

allez/tournez à gauche

allez tout droit

Prenez	la	première deuxième troisième	rue	à droite à gauche

> Many directions use the imperative, which you learnt about on pages 9–10.

Grammaire

On page 51 you saw how some determiners have to change after *à*, when it is used with *jouer*. It is the same pattern when *à* is used to say to a place:

Où est **le** musée? → Pour aller **au** musée?

Où sont **les** magasins? → Pour aller **aux** magasins?

Remember – *la* and *l'* do not change after *à*.

Vrai ou faux?

Read the directions below. Do they describe the route shown on the map correctly?

Allez tout droit puis prenez la deuxième rue à gauche. Continuez tout droit. Puis prenez la première rue à droite et l'église est à droite.

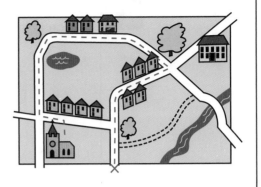

Key Point

You need to be able to ask your way to a place, *and* to give directions to someone, in speaking and in writing. You also need to be able to understand written directions.

Progress Check

Translate the following sentences into French:

1 What's the way to the castle?
2 Where is the Eiffel Tower?
3 Is there a swimming pool near here?
4 Is it far?
5 It's 100 metres away.

5 C'est à 100 mètres.
4 C'est loin?
3 Est-ce qu'il y a une piscine près d'ici?
2 Où est la Tour Eiffel?
1 Pour aller au château?

9.5 À la poste

There is a Musée de la Poste at Montparnasse in Paris. You can also visit its website:
www.museedelaposte.fr

Vocabulaire

Je voudrais envoyer	une lettre	en Angleterre
		en Écosse
	un colis	en Irlande du Nord
		au pays de Galles
	une carte postale	au Royaume-Uni

Je voudrais	un timbre	à	soixante-dix cents
	deux timbres		
	une télécarte		dix euros

Où est la boîte aux lettres, s'il vous plaît?

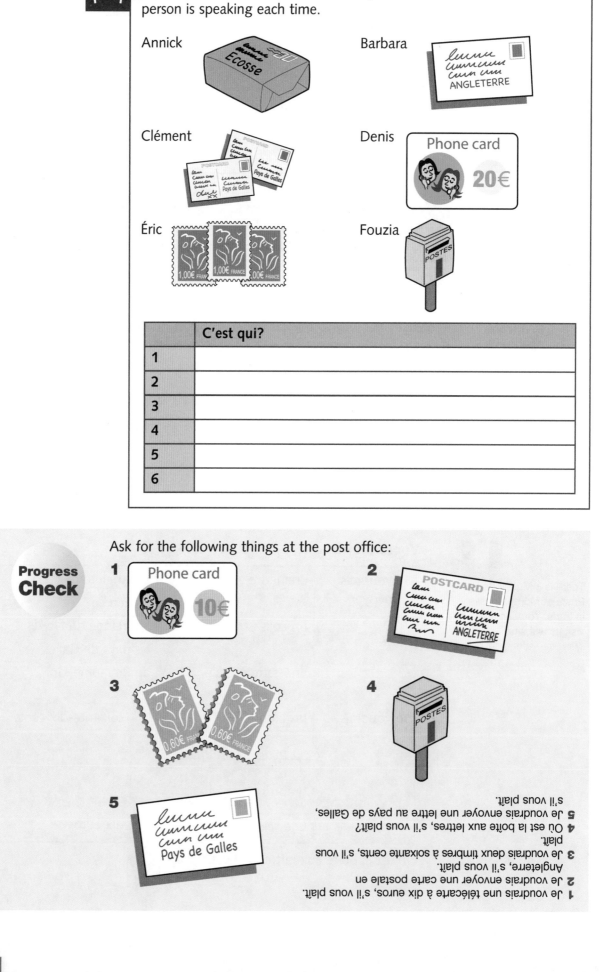

53 Écoutez et notez

Listen to these six conversations in a post office and work out which person is speaking each time.

Annick

Barbara
ANGLETERRE

Clément
Pays de Galles

Denis
Phone card
20€

Éric
1,00€ FRANCE 1,00€ FRANCE 1,00€ FRANCE

Fouzia
POSTES

	C'est qui?
1	
2	
3	
4	
5	
6	

Progress Check

Ask for the following things at the post office:

1 Phone card
10€

2 POSTCARD
ANGLETERRE

3 0.60€ FRANCE 0.60€ FRANCE

4 POSTES

5 Pays de Galles

1 Je voudrais une télécarte à dix euros, s'il vous plaît.
2 Je voudrais envoyer une carte postale en Angleterre, s'il vous plaît.
3 Je voudrais deux timbres à soixante cents, s'il vous plaît.
4 Où est la boîte aux lettres, s'il vous plaît?
5 Je voudrais envoyer une lettre au pays de Galles, s'il vous plaît.

J'aime lire!

Vous avez lu le livre.
Vous avez regardé le film.
Maintenant résolvez le mystère!

Pour décrypter le code Da Vinci, commencez à l'Hôtel du Ritz. Puis traversez les jardins des Tuileries pour aller au musée du Louvre. On peut y voir la peinture connue de Léonard de Vinci, *La Joconde*. Regardez aussi les deux pyramides en verre. Prenez la rue de Rivoli et les Champs-Élysées pour aller à l'église Saint-Sulpice. Ici se trouve la ligne Rose. Maintenant allez à la Gare du Nord et achetez un billet pour Lille. Mais plus tard il faut prendre le train pour aller au Château de Villette, près de Paris.

Find the mistake in this translation of the text.

You've read the book.
You've seen the film
Now solve the mystery!

To decrypt the Da Vinci code, start at the Ritz Hotel. Then cross the Tuileries Gardens to go to the Louvre museum. There you can see Leonardo da Vinci's famous painting, the *Mona Lisa*. Also look at the three glass pyramids. Take the Rue de Rivoli and the Champs-Élysées to go to the Saint Sulpice church. The Rose Line is situated here. Now go to the Gare du Nord and buy a ticket to Lille. But later you need to take the train to go to the Château de Villette, near Paris.

Mon dossier

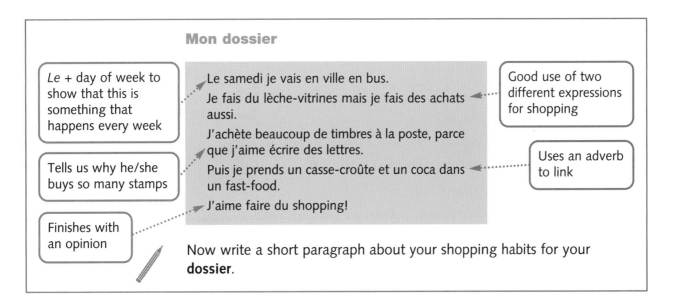

Le + day of week to show that this is something that happens every week

Le samedi je vais en ville en bus.
Je fais du lèche-vitrines mais je fais des achats aussi.
J'achète beaucoup de timbres à la poste, parce que j'aime écrire des lettres.
Puis je prends un casse-croûte et un coca dans un fast-food.
J'aime faire du shopping!

Good use of two different expressions for shopping

Tells us why he/she buys so many stamps

Uses an adverb to link

Finishes with an opinion

Now write a short paragraph about your shopping habits for your **dossier**.

Practice test questions

Listening 🎧 54

Tick the items the customer buys in the *charcuterie*, and the correct quantity of each. The first one has been done as an example.

	SALAD	MILK MILK	🔴	🍾	🔴	🍅	🧀	🍕
100g	✔							
250g								
500g								
1kg								
1 litre								
a bottle								
a piece								
a slice								

(7 marks)

Speaking

Ask for the following items at the post office.

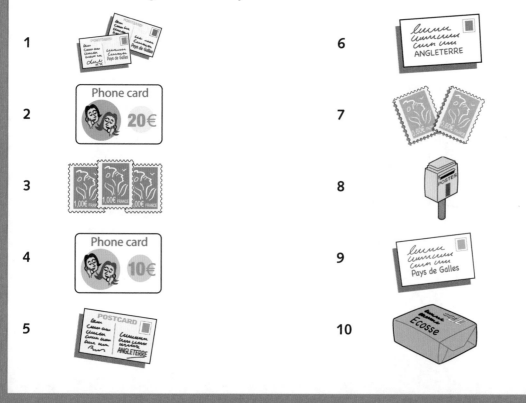

1

2

3

4

5

6

7

8

9

10

(10 marks)

Reading

Match these sentences about food preferences with the picture of the food they describe.

1 □   2 □   3 □

4 □   5 □   6 □

a	Je ne mange jamais de viande.	**d**	Ma sœur ne peut pas manger de blé parce qu'elle est allergique.
b	Mon père ne mange pas de sucre parce qu'il est diabétique.	**e**	Mon ami déteste le fromage et il ne le mange pas.
c	On est musulman, donc on ne mange pas de porc.	**f**	Je ne mange pas de cacahouètes parce que je suis allergique.

(6 marks)

Find the ordinal numbers in these sentences and write them in figures.

1 C'est la quatrième fois que je visite la France. _____

2 Un aller-retour en deuxième classe, s'il vous plaît. _____

3 Prenez la troisième rue à droite. _____

4 C'est la première à gauche. _____

5 Ma chaîne préférée est la cinquième. _____

6 Il habite au dixième étage. _____

7 J'arrive le premier août. _____

8 C'était au dix-huitième siècle. _____

9 Il est arrivé deuxième. _____

10 C'est son huitième voyage en Irlande. _____   **(10 marks)**

Writing

Write directions for how to get from the marked spot to the park.

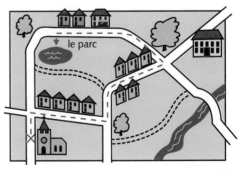

_____

_____

_____

_____

_____

(10 marks)

10 J'adore la techno

After studying this topic you should be able to:

- discuss your TV viewing habits and preferences
- recognise French text messages
- understand silent final letters and liaison in French pronunciation
- understand and use appropriate register in letter-writing and emails
- understand and use words about modern technology
- understand and write letters to a problem page

10.1 Téléfan

Écoutez et notez

55

Listen to the recording and note each speaker's favourite programme and the amount of TV they watch. Use the right-hand column to note any extra details.

	favourite programme	hours of TV per day	extra
1			
2			
3			
4			
5			
6			

In France there are six major TV channels available free of charge. France 2, France 3, Arte and La Cinqième are all national, public channels (a bit like BBC1 or BBC2). TF1 (Téléfrance 1) and M6 are commercial channels (like ITV1 or Channel 4 in the UK).

Vocabulaire

Qu'est-ce que tu aimes comme émission? – What kind of programmes do you like?

une émission – TV programme

une émission sportive/musicale/pour enfants – a sports/music/children's programme

une chaîne – a TV channel

un jeu (les jeux) – game show(s)

télé-réalité – reality TV

continuez >>>

<<< continuez

caméra cachée – hidden camera

un documentaire – documentary

une série – series, soap

les infos – the news

la météo – the weather forecast

Combien de temps regardes-tu la télé par jour? – How much TV do you watch every day?

Je regarde la télé une heure/deux heures par jour – I watch TV for 1 hour/2 hours per day

un fan/un fana/un fanatique – a fan, supporter

The French phrase *le programme de télé* is a 'false friend' (see page 29). It means the schedule of TV listings or guide (like the *Radio Times* magazine), not an individual TV programme (such as *Coronation Street*).

Grammaire

You can give a simple opinion just by using *j'aime* + a noun or infinitive. But to improve your performance in a speaking or writing exam, try to add more detail to your opinions, for example:

J'aime la télé

Vary the structure: **J'aime regarder** la télé.

Say when: J'aime regarder la télé **le week-end**.

Vary the word order: Le week-end, j'aime regarder la télé.

Give an alternative: Le week-end, j'aime regarder la télé **ou un film sur DVD**.

Add another clause: Le week-end, **quand j'ai le temps**, j'aime regarder la télé ou un film sur DVD.

Add another tense: Le week-end, quand j'ai le temps, j'aime regarder la télé ou un film sur DVD. La semaine dernière, **j'ai regardé** le Concours Eurovision de la Chanson.

And now add an opinion about Eurovision ...

Progress Check

Complete the names of these types of TV programme:

1 t____-r_____é (reality TV)

2 u___ é_____n p___r e_____s
(a children's programme)

3 c_____a c_____e (hidden camera)

4 u_ d_____e (a documentary)

5 l__ i____s (the news)

1 télé-réalité
2 une émission pour enfants
3 caméra cachée
4 un documentaire
5 les infos

10.2 Le langage texto

Le langage texto (or 'text-speak') is all the rage in France. You need to work hard on your French to understand it though. In particular, you need to know your French alphabet really well (see page 11).

Grammaire

A very important factor in French pronunciation is that not all the letters are pronounced. A good rule of thumb is that you don't usually pronounce the final letter of French words (particularly if they are followed by a word beginning with a consonant). This means that some words which look different when written are pronounced in a similar way:

dix (ten) ⟶ di~~x~~ ⎫
dit (says) ⟶ di~~t~~ ⎬ both sound like 'dee'
⎭

In English text-messaging people use letters, words and numbers to help shorten messages e.g. 'Don't b L8', 'C u 2nite' or 'RU OK'? Many young people in France also use this feature to help them shorten words in text messages.

deux (two) sounds like *de* (of), so both are shortened to 2

six (number six) sounds like *si* (if), so both are shortened to 6

crois (believe) sounds like *croix* (cross), so both are shortened to X

C sounds like *c'est* (it is) or *sais* (know)

G sounds like *j'ai* (I have)

Gt sounds like *j'étais* (I was)

Devinez puis écoutez

Guess the meaning of these text abbreviations – reading them aloud will help. (Try to do it without looking at the French answers in the box on the next page.) Then listen to the recording to check your answers.

	le langage texto	en français	in English
1	gt o 6né	J'étais au ciné(ma)	I was at the cinema
2	a2m1		See you tomorrow
3	c b1		That's good
4	c pa 5pa		That's not nice
5	g1id		I have an idea
6	ght1 kdo		I have bought a present

continuez >>>

<<< continuez

7	koi29		What's new?
8	gt nrv		I was irritated
9	gt oqp		I was busy
10	je c		I know
11	mr6		Thanks
12	ri1 29		nothing new

À demain   J'étais énervée

C'est bien   J'étais occupée

C'est pas sympa   Je sais

J'ai une idée   Merci

J'ai acheté un cadeau   Quoi de neuf?

~~J'étais au ciné(ma)~~   rien de neuf

C'est pas sympa is informal French. The correct phrase should be: ce **n'**est pas sympa. Part of the negative form is sometimes left out when speaking informally in French. For example, je **ne** sais pas is often shortened to je sais pas.

Grammaire

The final letters of some French words **are** pronounced when certain words are used together. This is called **liaison** (in both French and English) and means linking words together. It is best to learn the most common examples off by heart. For example:

dix minutes sounds like 'dee meenoot'

dix heures sounds like 'dees err'

Écoutez et notez

Listen to the recording and draw a line to mark the liaisons between the words. The first has been done as an example.

Exemple: Vous aimez les anciens élèves?

1   Je suis allé avec mes amis.

2   Il est son petit ami depuis un an.

3   J'ai plus ou moins le même âge.

4   Comment allez-vous?

5   Vous avez deux enfants?

6   David aime les escargots.

7   Nous en avons beaucoup.

8   Il n'y a rien à manger.

What are these common expressions in English?

1 J'étais occupé.

2 Quoi de neuf?

3 À demain.

4 J'ai une idée.

5 C'est bien.

1 I was busy.
2 What's new?
3 See you tomorrow.
4 I have an idea.
5 That's good.

10.3 Le courriel

Email and messaging services have been popular for a long time in France (longer than in the UK or the USA). Using email gives you a chance to say things that you might not dare to face to face!

Vocabulaire

la boîte aux lettres – mailbox

le courrier éléctronique

le courriel } email

le mèl

envoyer un courriel – to send an email

objet – subject line (in an email)

l'arobase (m) – 'at' sign in email addresses

point com – dot com

la connexion à Internet – Internet connection

Grammaire

Emails to a friend or someone you know well are usually informal and chatty. You could even use some of the same abbreviations as le langage texto. However, if you write an official letter or email, you would need to be more formal. This is called using the correct register. Saying vous to an adult is an example of formal register, whereas using tu with friends is an example of the informal register.

Part of letter/email	Formal	Informal
Greeting	Monsieur/Madame Cher Monsieur Chirac Chère Madame Lassalle	Salut! Cher Thierry, Chère Angelina, Chers amis,
Saying thank you	Je vous remercie d'avance Je vous remercie de vos renseignements	Je te remercie pour … Merci mille fois
Signing off	Je vous prie d'accepter, Monsieur/Madame, mes sentiments distingués. Veuillez agréer, Monsieur/Madame, mes sincères salutations.	Bien amicalement À bientôt Amitiés Grosses bises Je t'embrasse

Lisez et notez

Read the emails and find out who is writing about what.
Write the names into the spaces on page 130.

Objet: Feux d'artifice

Salut Mireille
Ça va?
Il y a des feux d'artifice en ville, samedi soir. Tu veux y aller avec moi?
Amitiés
Olivier

Objet: Concert
Chère Madame Dubois,
Merci pour l'invitation au concert la semaine prochaine, mais je ne peux pas accepter. Je ne peux pas venir, parce que je dois travailler.
Veuillez agréer, Madame Dubois, mes sincères salutations.
Gérard Andine

Objet: L'amour

Jacques
Je t'aime plus que jamais.
Avec tout mon amour,
Liliane

Objet: Mon anniversaire

Danielle
Merci bien pour le cadeau. C'est très joli mais pratique aussi.
À la prochaine!
Saïd

---

continuez >>>

<<< continuez

Objet: Bon rétablissement!

Marie-Noëlle

J'ai entendu dire que vous étiez malade.
J'espère que vous irez mieux bien vite.

Bien amicalement

Patricia

Objet: Je suis dans un cyber-café!

Salut Nourdine

En ce moment je suis en vacances à Nice.
Je m'amuse bien et donc je ne reste plus
longtemps dans ce cyber-café!

Bisous,

Zoë

Objet: Hervé de Villepin

Monsieur Laurent

Je suis désolée que Hervé n'était pas au
collège hier. Il va retourner au collège
demain.

Je vous prie d'agréer, Monsieur Laurent,
mes sentiments distingués.

Madame de Villepin

Objet: On rompt

Ahmed
Je ne veux plus sortir avec toi.
Sabrina

_____ is asking _____ out.

_____ is breaking up with _____.

_____ is ill.

_____ is in love with _____.

_____ is on holiday.

_____ is thanking _____ for a present.

_____ is turning down an invitation from _____.

_____ is writing an absence note for _____.

Key Point

You might have to write a short informal note, postcard or email
in the exam, so learn at least one greeting and one way to end
a letter off by heart. In Key Stage 3 you only have to understand
formal letters, not write them yourself.

Progress Check

Test yourself on this vocabulary:

1 To send an email

2 Inbox/letterbox

3 Dear (in an email or letter)

4 A formal way to say thank you

5 An informal end to a letter or email

1 envoyer un courriel
2 la boîte aux lettres
3 cher/chère
4 Je vous remercie (d'avance/de vos
renseignements)
5 Any one of: Bien amicalement/À
bientôt/Amitiés/Grosses bises/Je t'embrasse

10.4 On surfe!

With modern technology you will often see words used in different contexts as new terms have to be invented. If you are surfing online – *surfer sur Internet* – you will need to recognise the labels for hyperlinks used on French-language websites.

For some of these words, you will have to work out the meaning by looking at the context. This means looking at the sentence or paragraph in which the word is used. For example, *un portable* can be short for *un téléphone portable* (mobile phone) or *un ordinateur portable* (laptop). So if you meet the word *portable*, you have to read or listen to the rest of the sentence to work out which one is meant on this occasion:

Ton **portable** sonne – Your mobile is ringing

Je voudrais utiliser ton **portable** pour faire mes devoirs – I would like to use your laptop to do my homework

---

Trouvez dans le dictionnaire

Use a dictionary to find the conventional meaning of each word or phrase. Then match with its meaning on the Internet, taken from the box below.

	conventional meaning	meaning in technology
accueil (m)		
le bouton		
chercher		
fermer cette fenêtre		
un lien		
la recherche		
retour à la page précédente		
suite		

backward	forward	search
button	homepage	search
close this window	hyperlink	

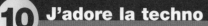

Find the two possible translations for each French word from the list below.

1 accueil

2 bouton

3 lien

4 retour

5 suite

backward, button, following, forward, homepage, hyperlink, link, spots, return, welcome

5 following, forward
4 backward, return
3 hyperlink, link
2 button, spots
1 homepage, welcome

10.5 Le courrier du cœur

Nom de plume literally means 'pen name'. Many people use a *nom de plume* when they write in to a newspaper or an agony aunt, as they want to keep their identity secret. This is often an adjective describing how you feel followed by the place you are from. The adjective should be preceded by *le* if you are a boy and *la* if you are a girl, and should agree with that gender, e.g. Le Laid / La Laide de Lyon – Ugly (boy/girl) of Lyon.

When you write a letter in French, put the name of the place you are writing from and the date, e.g. *Londres, le 25 décembre*, at the top right of the page.

un lecteur DVD – a DVD player

Vocabulaire

le courrier du cœur – problem page (literally, mail from the heart)

Ce n'est pas juste! – It's not fair!

Je n'ai jamais la permission – I never have permission

Je suis désespéré(e) – I am desperate/in despair

Je n'ai pas le droit – I do not have the right

Ils ne sont pas d'accord – They don't agree

Ils ne me comprennent pas – They don't understand me

Aidez-moi! – Help me!

Je ne sais pas quoi faire – I don't know what to do

Qu'est-ce que je peux faire? – What can I do?

J'ai besoin de votre conseil – I need your advice

Lisez et notez

Read these three letters written to an agony aunt, then decide whether each of the sentences below were written by either *La Désespérée de Dieppe* (DD), *Le Triste de Tours* (TT) or *La Malheureuse de Marseille* (MM).

Dieppe, le 29 janvier

Chère Margrite,

J'ai un problème. J'ai mis de l'argent de côté pendant quelques semaines et j'ai acheté un lecteur DVD. Je voudrais avoir le lecteur dans ma chambre, mais mes parents ont refusé. J'ai déjà une télévision. Pourquoi pas un lecteur aussi? Ce n'est pas juste!

La Désespérée de Dieppe

continuez >>>

<<< continuez

Tours, le 13 mars

Chère Margrite,

J'ai un problème. J'ai reçu de l'argent pour mon anniversaire et je veux acheter une console de jeux. Mais mes parents ne sont pas d'accord. Pourquoi??? Je voudrais m'amuser un peu. Je n'ai pas le droit d'acheter ce que je veux! Mais c'est mon argent!!!

Le Triste de Tours

Marseille, le 16 avril

Chère Margrite,

J'ai un problème. Nous n'avons pas d'ordinateur à la maison. Mes parents disent que c'est un luxe. Mais je crois qu'un ordinateur est essentiel! J'en ai besoin pour faire mes devoirs. Qu'est-ce que je peux faire? Aidez-moi!

La Malheureuse de Marseille

une console de jeux – a games console

		DD	TT	MM
1	I saved up my money for several weeks.			
2	I got loads of birthday money.			
3	I like to research things for my homework.			
4	My parents are infringing my rights.			
5	Things that our parents considered luxuries are essential nowadays!			
6	My parents are so unfair.			
7	I want to have a bit of fun.			
8	Why can I have one thing in my bedroom, but not the other?			

Key Point

If you are writing or speaking to someone in French you have to be careful to use the right register of language, formal or informal. It is also important to use the correct pronoun, *tu* or *vous*. If you are writing to an 'agony aunt', however, you can use the *tu* or the *vous* form.

Progress Check

Copy out these sentences with the words separated and with correct punctuation.

1 aidezmoi

2 cenestpasjuste

3 jaibesoindevotreconseil

4 jenesaispasquoifaire

5 questcequejepeuxfaire

5 Qu'est-ce que je peux faire?
4 Je ne sais pas quoi faire.
3 J'ai besoin de votre conseil.
2 Ce n'est pas juste!
1 Aidez-moi!

J'aime lire!

La publicité à la télé

Les plus grandes marques dépensent beaucoup d'argent pour faire de la publicité à la télé. On dit que la pub paie les émissions de bonne qualité. Mais qui paie la pub? Toi et moi, quand nous achetons ces produits!

Les pubs les plus connues sont aussi populaires que les émissions. Quelques téléfans préfèrent la pub aux émissions, parce qu'elles sont amusantes et mémorables.

La pub a une influence énorme. Par exemple, la musique de Moby et l'acteur Anthony Head sont devenus connus par la pub.

Les jeunes sont influencés par la publicité. La pub encourage les jeunes à acheter un produit. Dans quelques pays, la pub pour les enfants est interdite.

Les enfants très jeunes sont les plus impressionants. Ils ne comprennent pas que la pub est là pour vendre des produits. Ils pensent que c'est toujours leur émission préferée.

Part 1 – Prenez vos stylos!

You will need yellow, green, pink and blue highlighter pens for this activity. You know from the title that the text above is about advertising on the TV, so first of all:

- highlight all the words to do with advertising in yellow
- highlight all the words to do with television in pink

Now look at the remaining text:

- highlight all the cognates in blue
- highlight all the parts of *avoir* or *être* in green

You have now highlighted a large part of the text, before you even start to read it thoroughly. This should encourage you that even when faced with a complex French text, there is always quite a lot that you can identify immediately. Now you are ready for the second activity on this text.

Part 2 – Trouvez l'intrus

Read the text again, then find the opinion in the English summary below which did not appear in the original text.

- The big brands pay a lot of money for advertising on TV.
- Advertising on TV pays for high-quality programmes.
- Customers pay for the advertising.
- The best-known adverts are as popular as the TV programmes.
- Some viewers prefer the adverts to the TV programmes.
- TV advertising is very influential.

continuez >>>

<<< continuez

- In some countries the adverts last almost as long as the TV programmes.
- Appearing in TV adverts has boosted the careers of several big stars.
- Young people are encouraged to buy products by adverts.
- In some countries, adverts aimed at children are banned.
- Young children don't understand the difference between adverts and TV programmes.

Vocabulaire

la publicité/la pub – advertising

les grandes marques – big brands

sont devenus connus – became famous

interdit(e) – forbidden/banned

Grammaire

In French, superlatives, e.g. 'the best' or 'the smallest', are formed in the same way as the comparative (see page 78), but they have *le, la* or *les* before *plus* or *moins*:

les plus grandes marques – the most well-known brands

les pubs **les plus** connues – the most well-known adverts

Les enfants très jeunes sont **les plus** impressionants – Very young children are the most impressionable

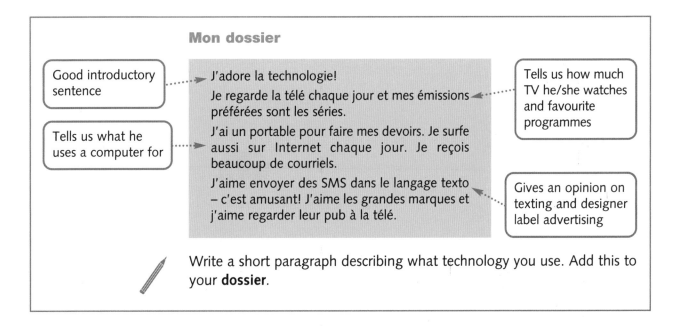

Mon dossier

Good introductory sentence

Tells us what he uses a computer for

J'adore la technologie!

Je regarde la télé chaque jour et mes émissions préférées sont les séries.

J'ai un portable pour faire mes devoirs. Je surfe aussi sur Internet chaque jour. Je reçois beaucoup de courriels.

J'aime envoyer des SMS dans le langage texto – c'est amusant! J'aime les grandes marques et j'aime regarder leur pub à la télé.

Tells us how much TV he/she watches and favourite programmes

Gives an opinion on texting and designer label advertising

Write a short paragraph describing what technology you use. Add this to your **dossier**.

Practice test questions

Listening 🎧 58

Listen to George talking about his use of technology. Note whether or not he likes or uses each type of technology.

		☺/☹
1	télévision	
2	la pub	
3	DVD	
4	ordinateur	
5	Internet	
6	courrier éléctronique	
7	portable	
8	SMS	
9	le langage texto	

(9 marks)

Speaking

Use the information shown to answer these questions about your television viewing habits.

1 Qu'est-ce que tu aimes comme émission?

2 Quelles émissions tu n'aimes pas?

3 Quelle est ta chaîne préférée?

4 Combien de temps regardes-tu la télé par jour?

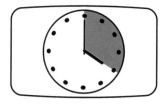

5 Tu regardes quelles séries?

(5 marks)

Reading

You are looking at some French websites with an English friend. Explain the French technical vocab to him.

1
> Accueil

2
> Chercher

3
> Cliquez ici

4
> Fermer cette fenêtre

5
> Liens utils

6
> Les résultats de votre recherche

7
> Retour à la page précédente

8
> Suite

(8 marks)

Writing

Complete this letter to a problem page, using the pictures to help you.

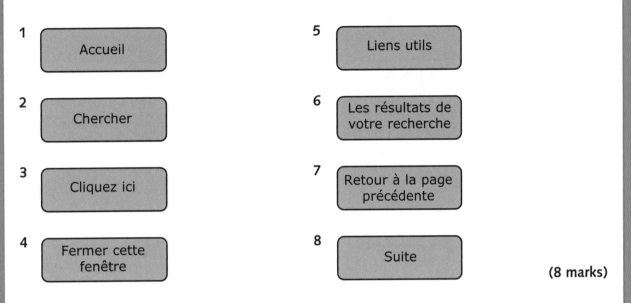

Besançon, le 24 mai

Chère Margrite,

J'ai un ☹ p_ _ _ _ _ _ _ _ _ _. J'ai des b_ _ _ _ _ _ _ _.

J_ v_ _ _ _ _ _ _ _ _ a_ _ _ _ _ _ _ _ u_ _ c_ _ _ _ _ antiseptique.

Mais m_ _ p_ _ _ _ _ _ _ ne sont pas d'accord. P_ _ _ _ _ _ _ _ _ _???

J'en ai b_ _ _ _ _ _ pour mes boutons. Malheureusement, je n'ai pas

d'a_ _ _ _ _ _ d_ p_ _ _ _ _. J_ n_ s_ _ _ _ p_ _ q_ _ _ _

f_ _ _ _ _ _. Aidez-m_ _ _!

Le Boutonneux de B_ _ _ _ _ _ _ _

(10 marks)

After studying this topic you should be able to:

- talk about your pocket money and how you spend it
- talk about part-time jobs
- form questions using a question word
- recognise and use indirect object pronouns
- use *aller* + infinitive to talk about future plans
- recognise and use the conditional
- use verbs with prepositions

11.1 L'argent de poche

Vocabulaire

l'argent (m) de poche – pocket money

Tu as combien d'argent de poche? –
How much pocket money do you get?

Je reçois 10 livres/15 euros par semaine – I get £10/15 euros per week

Qu'est-ce que tu fais avec ton argent?
– What do you do with your money?

Je dépense mon argent en … – I spend my money on …

J'achète – I buy

    vêtements – clothes

    DVDs – DVDs

    téléchargement de chansons – music downloads

    sorties – going out/trips

    activités sportives – sport

    produits de beauté – beauty products

    magazines – magazines

    jeux vidéos – video/computer games

    je paie mes appels sur mon portable – I pay for my mobile calls

Tu mets de l'argent de côté? – Do you save any money
(put money aside)?

Je fais des économies pour – I am saving for

    les vacances – the holidays

    pour acheter un portable/un vélo – to buy a mobile/bike

You could also talk about your pocket money in the past tense:

La semaine dernière j'ai reçu …/j'ai acheté … – Last week I received …/bought …

Writing or speaking in a variety of tenses helps to improve your mark in an exam.

continuez >>>

<<< continuez

Qui te donne ton argent de poche?
– Who gives you your pocket money?
Mes (grands-)parents me donnent ... – my (grand)parents give me ...
J'ai un petit boulot – I have a little job

Écoutez et notez

Listen to the four speakers and note the details of their pocket money.

	How much?	Who gives it?	Spends it on?	Saving?
1				
2				
3				
4				

Key Point

In listening tasks, the answers might not appear in the same order as the questions. Also, some boxes in the answer grid might be left blank.

Before listening to the recording, try to guess what the speaker might say. For example, in this listening task the answers to 'Spends it on?' might include: magazines, clothes, make up, music, mobile phone, books, trips and so on.

Grammaire

Indirect object pronouns are used to replace a noun when there are two objects in a sentence. The indirect object of the sentence is often preceded by 'to', so usually occurs with the verbs *donner* (to give), *offrir* (to give a present), *dire* (to say) and *montrer* (to show).

Indirect object pronouns:

me – to me   nous – to us
te – to you   vous – to you
lui – to him/to her   leur – to them

We often omit the word 'to' in English, for example:

Qui **te** donne ton argent de poche?

Who gives (to) you your pocket money?

The indirect object pronoun usually comes before the verb:

Ma mère **me** donne 10€ – My mother gives (to) me 10€

continuez >>>

<<< continuez

> Je **lui** montre son vélo – I show (to) them my bike
>
> Il **leur** dit la vérité – He is telling (to) them the truth

Indirect object pronouns are used in these common phrases:

> Pour mon anniversaire, on m'a offert ... – For my birthday, people gave me ...
>
> Je lui ai dit ... – I told him ...
>
> Il m'a expliqué ... – He explained to me ...

Progress Check

Underline the indirect object pronoun in each of these sentences, then translate into English.

1 Mes grands-parents te donnent 20 euros.

2 Le professeur m'a expliqué les devoirs.

3 Pour mon anniversaire, on m'a offert un nouveau portable.

4 Elle lui a montré ses devoirs.

5 Ils m'ont dit bonjour.

1 (te) My grandparents give you 20 euros.
2 (m') The teacher explained the homework to me.
3 (m') For my birthday, I got (people gave me) a new mobile.
4 (lui) She showed him her homework.
5 (m') They said hello to me.

11.2 Mon petit boulot

Vocabulaire

un petit boulot – part-time or temporary job

Tu commences/finis à quelle heure? – What time do you start/finish?

gagner – to earn

bien/mal payé – well/badly paid

pas mal – not bad

fatigant – tiring

deux/trois fois par semaine – two/three times per week

six (jours) sur sept – six (days) out of seven

je travaille	dans	un café
		un magasin
		un bureau
		un salon de coiffure
je fais	du jardinage (gardening)	
	du baby-sitting	
je distribue (I give out)	les prospectus (leaflets)	
	les journaux (newspapers)	

Grammaire

It is vitally important to be able to understand question words in French. Exam questions will very often be written in French, so you can't even begin to answer unless you understand the question!

combien? – how much/many?

comment? – how?

où? – where?

pourquoi? – why?

quand? – when?

qu'est-ce que? – what?

quel? – which?

qui? – who?

quoi? – what?

If *que* is followed by a vowel, the *e* is replaced by an apostrophe, but this does not happen with other question words:

Qu'est-ce que tu as? – What do you have?

Qui est arrivé? – Who has arrived?

The question words are often combined with other words to form more complicated questions:

Qui est-ce qui parle? – Who is it that is speaking?

De qui est-ce qu'il parle? – Who is he speaking about?

À qui est ce livre? – Whose book is this?

Quel is used with a noun to ask 'who?', 'which?' or 'what?'. It has to change depending on whether it is used with a masculine, feminine, singular or plural noun:

Quel est ton acteur préféré? – Who is your favourite actor? (masculine singular)

Quel**le** est ta matière préférée? – What's your favourite subject? (feminine singular)

Vous jouez de quels instruments? – Which instruments do you play? (masculine plural)

Quel**les** sont tes couleurs préférées? – What are your favourite colours? (feminine plural)

You often see quel used in exclamations:

Quel horreur! – How awful!

Quel dommage! – What a shame!

Quelle surprise! – What a surprise!

Quelle bonne idée! – What a good idea!

Key Point

Learn all the question words very carefully! Looking at the question word quickly gives you a good idea of what you have to do in an exam task. Also, revise the three different ways to form questions from ordinary sentences on page 36.

Écoutez et vérifiez

Work out what the correct question word is to complete each of these sentences, then listen to check your answer.

Aline

1 _____ est-ce que tu travailles le samedi?

   Je travaille dans un magasin de vêtements.

2 Tu commences à _____ heure?

   Je commence à neuf heures.

3 C'est _____ le travail?

   Pas mal. C'est intéressant et assez bien payé.

4 Tu gagnes _____?

   Je gagne 35 euros par jour.

5 _____ est-ce que tu vas au travail?

   J'y vais en autobus.

Guillaume

6 _____ est-ce que tu fais comme petit boulot?

   Je distribue les prospectus.

7 _____ est-ce que tu travailles?

   Je travaille le matin, six jours sur sept.

8 Tu gagnes _____? C'est bien payé?

   Non, pas du tout. Je gagne 35 euros par semaine.

9 _____ tu n'aimes pas ton boulot?

   Parce que c'est fatigant et ennuyeux.

Key Point

Aline and Guillaume don't actually say whether they like their part-time jobs or not. You have to work out their opinion from the other things they say. For example, Aline says her job is interesting and well paid. Guillaume thinks his job is boring, tiring and badly paid. You could be asked to infer information in this way in an exam.

Progress Check

Match each question with a suitable answer:

1 Tu gagnes combien?   a À midi.

2 Où est-ce que tu travailles?   b À pied.

3 Tu as un petit boulot?   c C'est assez bien payé.

4 Tu finis à quelle heure?   d Dans un salon de coiffure.

5 Comment vas-tu au travail?   e Oui, je fais du jardinage.

1 c, 2 d, 3 e, 4 a, 5 b

11.3 À l'avenir

According to a recent survey, a large proportion of children in France want to be professional footballers (22%) or singers (14%), whilst more than half intend to become teachers.

Vocabulaire

à l'avenir – in the future

terminer mes études – finish my studies

aller à l'université – go to university

faire un apprentissage – do an apprenticeship

faire une formation (en...) – to do training (in ...)

trouver un emploi – to find a job

travailler – to work

je vais être/je veux être ... – I will be/I want to be...

riche – rich	**content(e)** – happy
bien payé(e) – well-paid	**célèbre** – famous
marié(e) – married	

je vais avoir/je veux avoir ... – I will have/I want to have...

une grande maison – a large house

beaucoup d'argent – lots of money

beaucoup de temps libre – lots of free time

beaucoup d'enfants – lots of children

mes rêves/ambitions – my dreams/ambitions

voyager autour du monde – to travel around the world

gagner une médaille d'or aux Jeux Olympiques – to win an Olympic gold

gagner le Prix Nobel – to win the Nobel prize

me marier avec ... – to get married to ...

sortir chaque soir – to go out every evening

acheter – to buy

Grammaire

Talking about the near future is quite easy in French by using *aller* + an infinitive to say what you are *going* to do:

Je vais habiter au bord de la mer – I am going to live by the sea

On va faire un examen – We/they are going to do an exam

Je vais aller à la piscine – I am going to go to the swimming pool

Just take the correct part of the present tense of *aller* and add an infinitive:

je vais – I am going	nous allons – we go
tu vas – you are going	vous allez – you go
il/elle/on va – he/she/it/'one' goes	ils/elles vont – they go

Écoutez et lisez

Listen to these young people speaking about what they want to do in the future. Then write the right name next to each picture below. The first one has been done for you.

Élodie
Je vais quitter le lycée à l'âge de dix-huit ans. Puis je vais aller à l'université. Mon rêve est de gagner le Prix Nobel de science.

Arnaud
À l'avenir je vais faire un apprentissage en construction. Mon ambition est d'avoir une grande maison et beaucoup d'argent.

Yannick
En ce moment je prépare mon Bac. Je vais terminer mes études et puis je vais prendre une année sabbatique. Mon rêve est de voyager autour du monde. Je veux avoir beaucoup de temps libre.

Matthieu
Je vais quitter le collège à l'âge de seize ans. Je vais trouver un emploi. Je ne veux plus étudier et je veux sortir chaque soir.

Mélanie
Je vais me marier et je veux avoir beaucoup d'enfants. Mais d'abord je vais faire une formation dans un salon de beauté.

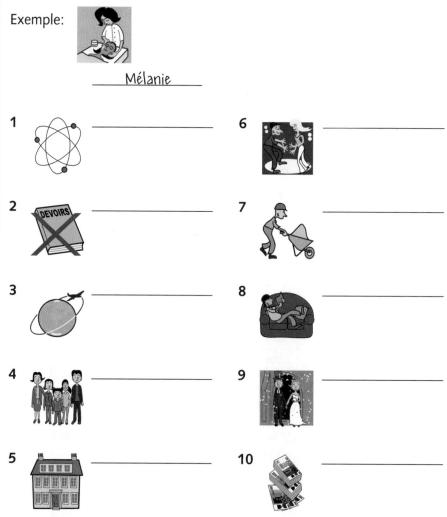

Exemple: Mélanie

1 _____

2 _____

3 _____

4 _____

5 _____

6 _____

7 _____

8 _____

9 _____

10 _____

Grammaire

Using *aller* + infinitive, as you saw above, is often called the near future, the simple future or the immediate future. To talk more generally about the future, you would use the future tense. This is formed by adding the following endings to the infinitive of the verb (removing the final -e first if necessary):

travailler – to work

je travailler**ai** – I will work

tu travailler**as** – you will work

il/elle/on travailler**a** – he/she/it/'one' will work

nous travailler**ons** – we will work

vous travailler**ez** – you will work

ils/elles travailler**ont** – they will work

It is important to remember that there is no separate word for 'will' in the future tense in French. You also need to learn some verbs which are irregular in the future:

je serai – I will be

j'aurai – I will have

j'irai – I will go

Key Point

In a speaking exam you might be asked to talk about your future plans. If you say you don't know or don't have any plans, you won't get many marks. It is better to use your imagination and say a few things you might do or would like to do in the future.

Progress Check

Match these sentences into logical pairs.

1 Je vais travailler comme médécin.

2 Je vais faire beaucoup de sport.

3 Je vais me marier avec Angelina Jolie.

4 Je vais avoir beaucoup d'enfants.

5 Je vais habiter à la montagne.

a Elle va divorcer.

b Je vais faire du ski.

c Je vais gagner une médaille aux Jeux Olympiques.

d Je vais habiter dans une grande maison.

e Je vais travailler dans un hôpital.

1 e, 2 c, 3 a, 4 d, 5 b

11.4 Mon stage

You are likely to do *un stage en entreprise* (work experience) in the near future. If not, this language can be used to talk about any training course (*un stage*) you would like to do.

> The conditional looks similar to the future tense, so take care not to mix them up. All verbs that are irregular in the future tense are also irregular in the conditional tense.

Grammaire

In the previous section you saw how the future tense and the near future with *aller* are used to talk about things you are reasonably certain are going to happen. The conditional is used to talk about things in the future that you are *not sure* will happen, or things that *might* happen.

Si j'avais de l'argent, **j'achèterais** une grande maison – If I had the money, I **would buy** a large house

You have already seen some conditionals used in earlier units:

Je **préférerais** rester à la maison – I would prefer to stay at home (Section 5)

Note that there is no separate word for 'would' in French. The conditional can be used with a noun or verb:

Je voudrais un café – I would like a coffee

Je voudrais regarder la télé – I would like to watch TV

Learn the following conditional verbs forms to use with infinitives:

je voudrais – I would like (I want)

j'aimerais – I would like (I would be happy)

je serais – I would be

j'aurais – I would have

je ferais – I would do

j'irais – I would go

je devrais – I should

Trouvez le numéro secret

Play the PIN game! Each phrase in the vocabulary box opposite has a number. Read the English sentence below and work out how you would say that in French. Then work out the code number for this phrase, e.g. 'I would like to work in a bank' ⟶ *Je voudrais travailler dans une banque* = 1, 2, 3.

1 I would like to work with computers.

2 I would like to work abroad.

3 In the future, I would like to go to university.

4 I would like to work outside, on a farm.

5 After my studies I would like to work with animals.

Vocabulaire

¹ je voudrais travailler	² dans	³ une banque ⁴ un bureau ⁵ un centre sportif ⁶ une école ⁷ une fabrique ⁸ une ferme ⁹ un hôpital ¹⁰ un magasin
	¹¹ avec	¹² des enfants ¹³ des animaux ¹⁴ des ordinateurs
	¹⁵ à	¹⁶ l'étranger (abroad) ¹⁷ l'extérieur (outside) ¹⁸ l'intérieur (inside) ¹⁹ la gare
²⁰ Un jour ²¹ Dans dix ans ²² À l'avenir ²³ Après mes études	²⁴ je voudrais	²⁵ aller à l'université ²⁶ faire un apprentissage ²⁷ préparer mon Bac ²⁸ travailler …

Progress Check

Match these conditional verb phrases to their translations:

1 j'aurais   **a** I would be
2 je ferais   **b** I would do
3 j'irais   **c** I would go
4 je serais   **d** I would have
5 je devrais   **e** I should

1 d, 2 b, 3 c, 4 a, 5 e

11.5 Bonnes intentions

As well as the future tense and the conditional, there are other ways to talk about your plans and intentions in French. You have already met several structures where a verb in French can be followed by an infinitive. Sometimes the two verbs have to be separated by the preposition à or de.

Je commence **à** manger plus sainement – I am starting to eat more healthily

J'ai décidé **de** devenir astronaute – I have decided to become an astronaut

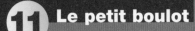

The second verb in each pair usually remains in the infinitive, but the first verb can be used in any tense. These are the verbs and prepositions you are most likely to use. (You might also see them used with other prepositions.)

apprendre à – to learn to

arrêter de – to stop

continuer à – to continue to

commencer à – to start

décider de – to decide to

essayer de – to try to

refuser de – to refuse to

Traduisez en français

Use the table below to translate the sentences into French:

j'ai décidé de	devenir végétarien(ne)
j'apprends à	nager
j'essaie de	boire du coca
j'ai arrêté de	manger plus sainement
je commence à	faire mes devoirs
je refuse de	fumer des cigarettes

1 I am learning to eat more healthily.

_____

2 I have decided to become a vegetarian.

_____

3 I am trying to do my homework.

_____

4 I refuse to smoke cigarettes.

_____

5 I have stopped drinking cola.

_____

6 I am starting to swim.

_____

Key Point These phrases could be useful in several different contexts, for instance talking about a healthy lifestyle, New Year's resolutions, your plans for the future, improving your grades at school, and so on.

Progress Check

Choose the correct preposition for each of these verb phrases.

1 J'ai décidé _____ devenir professeur.

2 J'apprends _____ nager.

3 J'essaie _____ manger moins de chocolat.

4 J'ai arrêté _____ faire mes devoirs.

5 Je refuse _____ manger de la viande.

5 de
4 de
3 de
2 à
1 de

Une manie des sondages! – crazy about surveys!

ils ne font que – they do nothing but

J'aime lire!

Une manie des sondages!

Tout le monde fait des sondages! Les journalistes adorent les sondages, parce qu'ils sont faciles à écrire. Il y a beaucoup de gens qui travaillent dans le marketing, et **ils ne font que** des sondages. À l'école on fait des sondages tout le temps. Même le gouvernement fait un énorme sondage – le recensement de la population. Alors, je vais faire un sondage au sujet des sondages:

Qu'est-ce que tu penses des sondages?

a Je les adore (je suis journaliste).

b Je les déteste.

c C'est quoi, un sondage?

d Non, non, non, je ne fais plus de sondages!

Activité

The author mentions different types of surveys. Put a tick by the four surveys NOT mentioned in the original text.

a Surveys in newspapers ☐

b Surveys on TV ☐

c Surveys trying to sell you something ☐

d Marketing surveys ☐

e The population census ☐

f Surveys at school ☐

g Health surveys ☐

h A survey about surveys ☐

i Traffic surveys ☐

Mon dossier

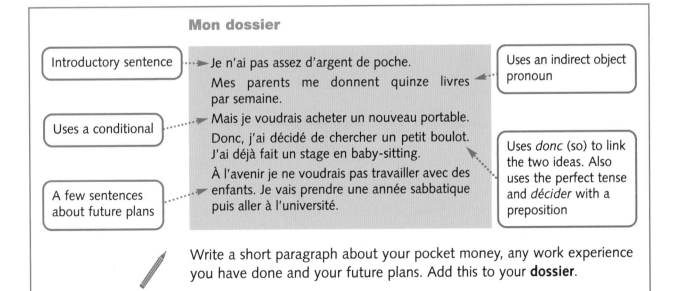

Introductory sentence ····➤ Je n'ai pas assez d'argent de poche.

Mes parents me donnent quinze livres par semaine. ◄···· Uses an indirect object pronoun

Uses a conditional ····➤ Mais je voudrais acheter un nouveau portable.

Donc, j'ai décidé de chercher un petit boulot. J'ai déjà fait un stage en baby-sitting.

À l'avenir je ne voudrais pas travailler avec des enfants. Je vais prendre une année sabbatique puis aller à l'université. ◄···· A few sentences about future plans

Uses *donc* (so) to link the two ideas. Also uses the perfect tense and *décider* with a preposition

 Write a short paragraph about your pocket money, any work experience you have done and your future plans. Add this to your **dossier**.

Practice test questions

Listening 🎧 62

Listen to Véronique talking about her part-time job and tick the correct answer. The first one has been done for you.

Exemple:

Elle s'appelle …   **a** Véronique ✔   **b** Angélique ☐   **c** Frédérique ☐

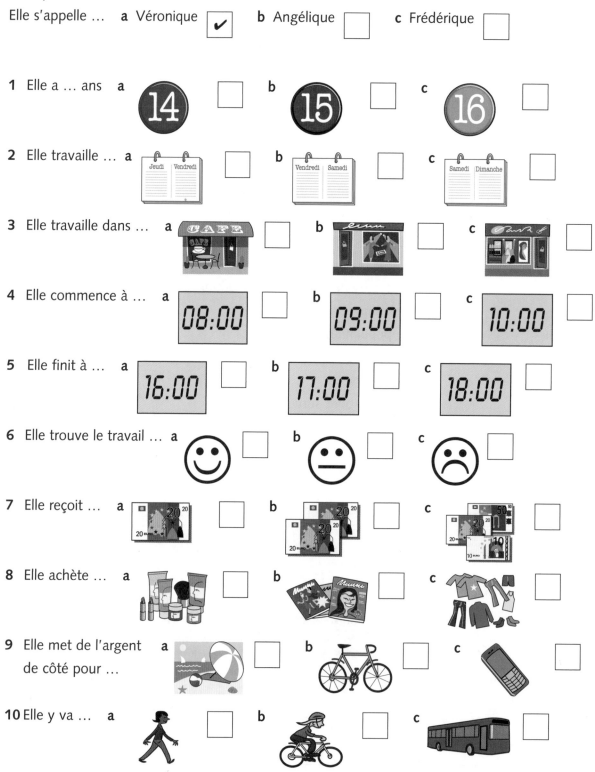

1 Elle a … ans   **a** 14 ☐   **b** 15 ☐   **c** 16 ☐

2 Elle travaille …   **a** Jeudi Vendredi ☐   **b** Vendredi Samedi ☐   **c** Samedi Dimanche ☐

3 Elle travaille dans …   **a** ☐   **b** ☐   **c** ☐

4 Elle commence à …   **a** 08:00 ☐   **b** 09:00 ☐   **c** 10:00 ☐

5 Elle finit à …   **a** 16:00 ☐   **b** 17:00 ☐   **c** 18:00 ☐

6 Elle trouve le travail …   **a** ☐   **b** ☐   **c** ☐

7 Elle reçoit …   **a** ☐   **b** ☐   **c** ☐

8 Elle achète …   **a** ☐   **b** ☐   **c** ☐

9 Elle met de l'argent de côté pour …   **a** ☐   **b** ☐   **c** ☐

10 Elle y va …   **a** ☐   **b** ☐   **c** ☐

(10 marks)

Speaking

Answer the survey questions as shown in full sentences.

1  Tu as combien d'argent de poche?

2 Qui te donne ton argent de poche?

3 Tu aides à la maison?

4 Qu'est-ce que tu fais avec ton argent?

5 Tu mets de l'argent de côté?

(5 marks)

Reading

Match the pairs of sentences.

1 Je vais aller à l'université.

2 Je vais avoir beaucoup d'argent.

3 Je vais avoir une grande famille.

4 Je vais faire un apprentissage.

5 Je vais gagner une médaille aux Jeux Olympiques.

6 Je vais quitter le collège aussitôt que possible.

7 Je veux devenir pharmaciste.

8 Je vais travailler dans une école.

9 Je vais travailler dans une ferme.

10 Je vais voyager autour du monde.

a J'adore le sport.

b J'aime passer des examens et faire mes études.

c J'aime les animaux.

d J'aime les enfants.

e Je déteste étudier.

f Je vais prendre une année sabbatique.

g Je veux devenir professeur.

h Je veux être bien payé.

i Je veux faire une formation.

j Je vais travailler dans un hôpital.

(10 marks)

Writing

Write sentences in French for these good intentions.

1 I'm learning to swim. _____

2 I'm continuing to eat more healthily. _____

3 I have decided to look for a part-time job. _____

4 I refuse to smoke. _____

5 I have stopped drinking cola. _____

6 I'm starting to do my homework. _____

7 I'm trying to become vegetarian. _____

8 I have decided to become a teacher. _____

9 I'm trying to eat less chocolate. _____

10 I'm continuing to do more sport. _____

(10 marks)

After studying this topic you should be able to:

- know more about francophone countries and their festivals
- use prepositions with countries and dates
- understand and use greetings for special occasions
- use a variety of tenses

12.1 Les pays francophones

Écoutez et lisez

Environ cent soixante millions de gens dans le monde parlent français. On parle français comme langue maternelle ou langue officielle dans quarante-quatre pays et sur quatre continents. En Europe, une partie des Belges et des Suisses parle français. En Amérique du Nord on parle français en Louisiane et au Canada. En Amérique du Sud on parle français aux Antilles et à Haïti. En Afrique on parle français dans une vingtaine de pays. Même en Asie, on parle français au Laos, au Cambodge et au Viêt-nam. Dans d'autres pays, le nombre de gens qui apprennent le français a augmenté de plus de vingt pour cent dans ces dix dernières années.

Now underline the names of all the countries in the text.

Grammaire

It is easy enough to understand the names of most countries in French – they are generally very similar to the English. What is more difficult is learning the correct preposition to use with each, to say 'to' or 'in' that country. Which preposition you use depends on whether the country is masculine, feminine or plural.

Use **au** with masculine singular countries and **en** with feminine singular countries. For plurals, use **aux**.

J'habite …

Je vais …

	Masculine	Feminine
Singular	**au** Mexique	**en** Grèce
Plural	**aux** États-Unis	**aux** Antilles

continuez >>>

<<< continuez

Small islands are generally feminine and you use **à** with them.

Je vais
- à la Martinique
- à la Réunion
- à l'Île Maurice

Use **en** with continents:

Je vais en Amérique du Sud.

Écoutez et notez

64

Listen to the recording and write the Internet domain name suffix for each francophone country into the column on the right. The first has been done as an example.

Pays	suffixe du nom de domaine
Belgique	.be
Burkina Faso	
Cambodge	
Cameroun	
Canada	
Congo	
Côte d'Ivoire	
France	
Laos	
Luxembourg	
Mali	
Madagascar	
Sénégal	
Tchad	
Tunisie	

Mauritius (Île Maurice) is a small island in the south-west Indian Ocean. It was a former French colony and so French is still spoken there. The islands Martinique and Reunion are both French *départements* (counties) even though Martinique is in the Caribbean and Reunion is in the Indian Ocean!

What is the correct preposition to say **in** or **to** each of these countries?

Progress Check

1 Canada (m)

2 France (f)

3 Martinique (f)

4 Maroc (m)

5 Seychelles (pl)

5 aux Seychelles
4 au Maroc
3 à la Martinique
2 en France
1 au Canada

12.2 L'année en France

The French love a festival! Almost every month there is a celebration, with even more in spring and summer when many towns have their own local celebrations. Some French people are even beginning to adopt American celebrations such as Halloween, too!

Écoutez et vérifiez

Guess in which month each of these festivals take place in France. Copy the months from the list below into the gaps, then listen to the recording to check your answers.

| janvier | février | mars | avril | mai | juin | juillet | août |
| septembre | octobre | novembre | décembre |

le 1er _____	le jour de l'An
le 14 _____	la Saint Valentin
le 1er _____	poisson d'avril
le 1er _____	la fête du travail
le 14 _____	la fête nationale
_____	vacances!
la première semaine de _____	la rentrée des classes
le 31 _____	Halloween
le 31 _____	la Saint-Sylvestre/le réveillon

Vocabulaire

la fête – celebration, party, religious festival

le poisson d'avril – April fool

la rentrée (des classes) – back to school

le réveillon – midnight celebration to see in the New Year

Grammaire

- Months, days of the week and seasons in French are always masculine and are written with a small letter
- To say 'in' a month, use *en*
- To say 'in' a season use *en*, except for spring:
  au printemps, **en** été, **en** automne, **en** hiver
- To say what the date is, use *c'est le*. If it is the first of the month, use *premier*:
  c'est le premier septembre
- For all other days in a month, just use the number (not an ordinal):
  c'est le quatorze février
  c'est le trente et un octobre
- If you want to say the day of the week as well, leave out the determiner:
  c'est vendredi treize octobre
- To answer the question: Quelle est la date de ton anniversaire? – When is your birthday?:
  Mon anniversaire, c'est le … (vingt-cinq décembre)
- To say in a year, use *en*:
  je suis né en 1995
- For years from 2000 onwards, say 'two thousand' first, then the other numbers :
  2011 ⟶ deux mille onze
- For years until 1999, say the thousand first, then the hundreds (without an s), and then the other years:
  1960 ⟶ mille neuf cent soixante

Key Point

If you know about French culture and other francophone countries, you will find it easier to do exercises like the one in this chapter.

Progress Check

1 What do the French call their national holiday?

2 When is it celebrated?

3 What is *la rentrée*?

4 What is *un poisson d'avril*?

5 When is *la Saint-Sylvestre*?

1 la fête nationale
2 Fourteenth July
3 First week of September when everyone goes back to school
4 April fool
5 Thirty-first December/New Year's Eve

12.3 On fait la fête!

 Le 1ᵉʳ janvier, c'est **le jour de l'An**. On célèbre le départ d'une nouvelle année.

 **Le vendredi 13**, pour certains, c'est une journée pleine de misères et de malchance. Mais les autres pensent qu'on aura plus de chance que d'habitude.

 Le dernier dimanche de mai c'est **la fête des Mères**. On offre une carte et un cadeau à maman pour dire merci.

 Durant le mois du **Ramadan** les musulmans ne mangent pas pendant la journée. Après un mois on fête la fin du Ramadan: l'Aïd-al-Fitr.

 En mars ou avril, c'est **Pâques**. On offre du chocolat et les enfants cherchent les œufs dans le jardin pour célébrer le printemps.

 Le 25 décembre, c'est bien sûr le jour de **Noël**, quand on fête la naissance du Christ. On décore un sapin de Noël et on offre des cadeaux.

 Le 14 juillet, c'est **la fête nationale**. On fête la révolution française. Dans chaque ville il y a un défilé et des feux d'artifice.

 Le **Hannoucah:** Vers la fin de l'ánnée les juifs célèbrent la fête de la lumière. Pendant huit jours on allume des bougies.

 La première semaine de septembre c'est **la rentrée** des classes. Tout le monde rentre à l'école. Quelquefois les parents offrent une nouvelle trousse avec des stylos et des crayons.

Vocabulaire

on célèbre/on fête – we/they celebrate

on offre (des fleurs) – we/they give (flowers) as a present

un défilé – a parade

les feux d'artifice – fireworks

les musulmans – Muslims

la naissance – birth

un sapin – fir tree

un cadeau – present, gift

on allume des bougies – we/they light candles

Vrai, faux ou on ne sait pas?

Read the descriptions of the celebrations on the previous page and decide whether each statement below is true (✔), false (✘) or not in the text (?).

		✔ / ✘ / ?
Exemple	People celebrate New Year by singing traditional songs	?
1	In France, Mother's Day is the last Sunday in May	
2	At Easter, children search for chocolate	
3	On their national holiday, the French have parades and fireworks	
4	In France, children have to buy all the text books and exercise books they use themselves	
5	Some people in France think they have better luck on Friday 13th	
6	Ramadan lasts a month	
7	People in France don't usually have Christmas trees	
8	Hanukkah lasts nine days	

Grammaire

Many sentences in this section use *on* to talk about festivals, e.g. *on fête Noël*. This can mean: '**We** celebrate Christmas' or '**They** celebrate Christmas'.

This means that you can use the vocabulary in this section to describe a festival that you, personally, celebrate or someone else's celebrations.

Learn to describe something that you celebrate with your family. As well as using the vocabulary in this section, you could think up some sentences about what you eat, wear and sing, or anything special that happens, such as dancing or fireworks, e.g.

Dans ma famille on célèbre – In my family we celebrate

C'est une fête importante en Angleterre/dans la religion – It's an important festival in England/in the … religion

Progress Check

Test yourself on this vocabulary:

1 on offre

2 on fête

3 les bougies

4 le sapin de Noël

5 les feux d'artifices

5 fireworks
4 Christmas tree
3 candles
2 we/they celebrate
1 we/they give (as a present)

12.4 Cartes de vœux

You can buy a greetings card (une carte de vœux) for almost every occasion nowadays. They are becoming almost as popular in France as they are in the English-speaking world.

As well as celebrating birthdays, many Roman Catholic families celebrate their *fête*, which is the saint's day whose name they share. Many people send cards on name days and wish the person celebrating: *Très bonne fête!*

Écoutez et notez

66

Listen to the people giving congratulations in French. Find the correct greetings card for that occasion and write the number into the box beside.

1 ☐   2 ☐   3 ☐   4 ☐

5 ☐   6 ☐   7 ☐

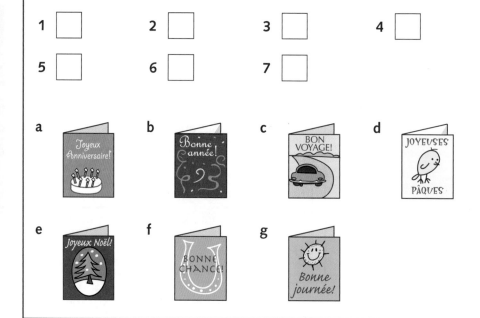

a *Joyeux Anniversaire!*

b *Bonne année!*

c BON VOYAGE!

d JOYEUSES PÂQUES

e *Joyeux Noël!*

f BONNE CHANCE!

g *Bonne journée!*

Key Point

If you want to congratulate someone or give your best wishes for any occasion, you can say:

meilleurs vœux – best wishes

félicitations – congratulations.

There is no simple rule for when you use each word, so just learn idioms as you meet them:

j'ai quatorze **ans**

l'année dernière.

Grammaire

Some time periods have more than one word to describe them in French:

an/année – year	jour/journée – day
matin/matinée – morning	soir/soirée – evening

Progress Check

Wish someone all the best in French on these occasions.

1 Happy New Year

2 Good luck!

3 Have a good day

4 Happy Birthday

5 Merry Christmas

1 Bonne année!
2 Bonne chance!
3 Bonne journée!
4 Joyeux Anniversaire!
5 Joyeux Noël!

12.5 Joyeux anniversaire

Écoutez et lisez

Normalement pour fêter mon anniversaire je vais dans un restaurant avec ma famille. Ma famille m'offre beaucoup de cadeaux et on mange bien. Mais cette année je voulais le fêter avec mes amis. J'ai organisé une petite fête pour vingt amis. J'ai acheté des chips et des boissons, j'ai choisi la musique et j'ai rangé la maison après la soirée. Je me suis bien amusée mais c'était beaucoup de travail. L'année prochaine je voudrais faire moins d'effort et je vais aller dans un restaurant encore!

Now underline all the time expressions.

Key Point

It is important to be able to use a variety of tenses in all the topics you write and speak about. In some writing exams you might have to describe what you did recently, what you are doing today and what you are going to do at the weekend to get the highest marks. This is not as difficult as it sounds, as you only need to learn a few key verbs, such as *avoir, être, faire* and *aller*, to be able to describe lots of things you do in the past, present or future.

It is important to recognise time expressions when you see or hear them as these indicate which tense is being used.

Make sure you learn a variety of them that you use often in your own speaking and writing:

past	present	future
hier	aujourd'hui	demain
hier matin	ce matin	demain matin
l'année dernière	cette année	l'année prochaine
la semaine dernière	cette semaine	la semaine prochaine
déjà	maintenant	à l'avenir

As well as time expressions, try to learn these frequency expressions that can be used in any tense to say how often something happens:

toujours – always/still

souvent – often

quelquefois – sometimes

rarement – rarely/not often

une fois par semaine – once a week

Remplissez les blancs

Complete the table with the first person singular (the *je* form) perfect tense, present tense and near future form of each verb (they are all verbs you could use to describe holidays or parties).

Infinitive	Perfect tense	Present tense	Future
acheter (to buy)	j'ai acheté	j'achète	je vais acheter
manger (to eat)			
écouter (to listen to)			
parler (to talk)			
faire (to do, make)			
aller (to go)	je suis allé(e)	je vais	
s'amuser (to have fun)	je me suis amusé(e)		je vais m'amuser

Progress Check

Say whether each of these time expressions is past, present or future:

1 cette semaine

2 demain matin

3 la semaine dernière

4 déjà

5 aujourd'hui

5 present
4 past
3 past
2 future
1 present

J'aime lire!

Le Sénégal

Le Sénégal est un assez petit pays dans l'ouest de l'Afrique, sur la côte Atlantique. La capitale, Dakar, est connue pour le rallye Paris–Dakar chaque année. Il y a un climat tropical et il fait assez chaud toute l'année. On exporte les cacahouètes, le poisson et la musique. (Le chanteur Youssou N'Dour est sénégalais.) La population est de douze millions, et on parle français, wolof et d'autres langues africaines. La majorité des gens sont musulmans. Le 4 avril, c'est la fête nationale et on célèbre l'indépendance. On fête aussi toutes les fêtes musulmanes et le nouvel an.

continuez >>>

<<< continuez

Now fill in a travel guide for Senegal.

Country	Senegal
Capital	
Location	
Climate	
Exports	
Population	
Languages	
Religion	
Events	

Mon dossier

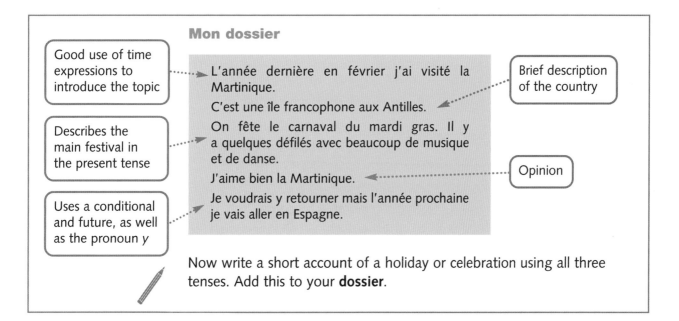

Good use of time expressions to introduce the topic

Describes the main festival in the present tense

Uses a conditional and future, as well as the pronoun *y*

L'année dernière en février j'ai visité la Martinique.
C'est une île francophone aux Antilles.
On fête le carnaval du mardi gras. Il y a quelques défilés avec beaucoup de musique et de danse.
J'aime bien la Martinique.
Je voudrais y retourner mais l'année prochaine je vais aller en Espagne.

Brief description of the country

Opinion

Now write a short account of a holiday or celebration using all three tenses. Add this to your **dossier**.

Practice test questions

Listening 🎧 68

Work out what these people are doing and when and complete the table in English.

	When	Activity
Exemple	yesterday morning	listened to music
1		
2		
3		
4		
5		
6		
7		
8		
9		
10		

(20 marks)

Speaking

Wish a French friend ...

1 Happy Birthday!

2 Merry Christmas!

3 Good luck!

4 Have a good journey!

5 Happy New Year!

6 Have a good day!   **(6 marks)**

Reading

Read these descriptions of two festivals celebrated by some Christians in France – Epiphany or the Feast of Kings (la fête des Rois), and Candlemas (Chandeleur). Then complete the English translation.

Le six janvier on fête la fête des Rois. On mange une galette avec une fève cachée.
Si on trouve la fève, on est roi ou reine pour la journée.

On fête la Chandeleur quarante jours après Noël. Selon la tradition, on fait des crêpes.

People in France celebrate the Epiphany on _____. People _____
a special cake which contains a _____ charm. The person who finds the charm is
king or queen _____ _____ _____.

Candlemas takes place _____ _____ _____ Christmas.
_____ to tradition, people _____ _____.   **(12 marks)**

Read this passage, then fill in the travel guide below.

La Martinique

La Martinique est une petite île aux Antilles (la mer des Caraïbes). La capitale s'appelle Fort-de-France. Il y a un climat tropical et il fait assez chaud toute l'année. On exporte des bananes, du sucre et du café. La population est de quatre cent mille habitants. On parle français et créole patois. La majorité des gens sont catholiques. La Martinique est une partie de la France, et donc on fête la fête nationale le 14 juillet. On fête aussi le carnaval à la fin de l'hiver.

Martinique	
Capital	
Location	
Climate	
Exports	
Population	
Languages	
Religion	
Events	

(8 marks)

Writing

Match up the two halves of these sentences to complete this description of how one family celebrates Christmas.

Exemple: Dans ma religion on célèbre _____
1 Le 25 décembre, c'est _____ *la naissance du Christ* _____
2 C'est une fête importante en _____
3 Dans ma famille on _____
4 On offre des _____
5 Le soir on allume _____
6 On décore _____
7 Normalement, il n'y a pas de _____

~~la naissance du Christ.~~	Grande-Bretagne.
cadeaux.	le jour de Noël
des bougies.	s'amuse bien.
feux d'artifices.	un sapin de Noël.

(7 marks)

Description of NC levels

These descriptions help you understand what you have to do to reach a particular National Curriculum level in each skill. The full text of these levels can be found online at: http://www.qca.org.uk/downloads/3804_mfl_level_desc.pdf

	Listening	Speaking	Reading	Writing
	I can understand…	I can…	I can understand…	I can…
Level 1	short, everyday instructions, comments and questions	say a few words or short phrases	single French words, possibly with the help of a picture	copy familiar words correctly
Level 2	familiar statements and questions	ask and answer simple questions, ask for help and make myself understood	short phrases, and find the meaning of new words in a glossary	copy familiar phrases correctly and write a few words from memory
Level 3	short, familiar passages such as messages and conversations at near normal speed; I can note main points and some details	ask and answer at least two or three questions from memory; I can say what I like or dislike and how I feel	short texts of familiar language; I can note main points including feelings and look up new words in a French–English dictionary	write two or three sentences with the help of my books; I can write about my feelings and also short phrases from memory with reasonable accuracy
Level 4	longer passages of simple sentences; I can note main points and some details	take part in a conversation of at least four exchanges, changing phrases I have learnt to say what I want	different kinds of short texts, both printed and handwritten; I can note main points and some details and work out the meaning of some words I have not met before	write a short paragraph of three or four sentences, mostly from memory; I can write my own sentences by changing words and phrases; I use a dictionary to check spellings
Level 5	familiar language from several topics, including present and **either** past **or** future events; I can note main points and specific details, including opinions	take part in short conversations, asking for and giving information and simple opinions; I can talk about recent experiences **or** future plans, as well as everyday events	a range of written material including present and **either** past **or** future events; I can note main points and specific details, including opinions; I can understand some real French texts using a dictionary	produce short pieces of writing, asking questions, giving information and opinions; I can write about recent experiences **or** future plans, as well as everyday events; I can use a dictionary to look up new words
Level 6	short narratives of present, past **and** future events spoken at normal speed; I can understand familiar language in unfamiliar contexts and identify specific details	take part in conversations that include present, past **and** future events; I can use my knowledge of grammar to talk about new contexts (as well as familiar ones)	texts covering present, past **and** future events, including language I know in new situations; I can use my knowledge of grammar and context to help work out language I have not met before	write longer paragraphs, referring to present, past **and** future events; I can use my knowledge of grammar to write my own sentences
Level 7	a range of material and complex sentences including material taken from radio and TV	start and develop conversations and discuss various topics in a variety of tenses	a range of factual and imaginative texts that includes some complex sentences and unfamiliar language	write about a variety of topics in different registers; I can link sentences and adapt familiar language for my own purposes
Level 8	spoken material from a range of sources such as films and plays; I can recognise attitudes and emotions from familiar and unfamiliar material	justify my opinions in a range of vocabulary and structures; I can adapt language to deal with unprepared conversations	a wide variety of written texts, including unfamiliar topics and more complex language	express and justify my ideas and seek the views of others
Exceptional performance	a wide range of factual and imaginative speech and summarise and report it in detail	discuss a wide range of factual and imaginative topics in informal and formal situations	a wide range of texts including official and formal language; I can summarise in detail as well as report and explain texts	write accurately about a wide range of factual and imaginative topics, varying the form and style

Answers

Unit 1 Allez-y!

p.6 Reliez les questions et les réponses

1 b; **2** a; **3** d; **4** c; **5** e

p.9 Écoutez et cochez

	Tu	Vous
Exemple	✓	
1	✓	
2		✓
3		✓
4	✓	
5	✓	
6		✓

p.10 Cherchez dans le dictionnaire

le dictionnaire – dictionary
la faute – mistake
la feuille – sheet (of paper)
le mot – word
le nom – noun or name
la page – page
la phrase – sentence
la réponse – answer
la traduction – translation
le verbe – verb

p.11 Cherchez le digramme

sœur pages 32, 33, 34, 36, 42, 44, 45, 55, 59, 78, 80, 83.
œil p.101; hors d'œuvres p.115, 116
cœur p.132
œufs p.156
vœux p.158

p.12 Écoutez et écrivez

1 Jeanne d'Arc
2 Zinédine Zidane
3 L'empereur Napoléon
4 Céline Dion
5 Astérix et Obélix
6 Yves Saint Laurent

p.12 Écoutez et lisez

Chloé; she speaks French, German and Italian.

p.15 Écoutez et cochez

	Pronounced differently	Pronounced the same
Exemple	✓	
1	✓	
2	✓	
3	✓	
4	✓	
5		✓
6	✓	
7		✓
8	✓	
9		✓
10	✓	

p.15 J'aime lire

1 a; **2** c; **3** b

Practice Test Questions

p.16 Listening

1 Angélique Laurent
2 Félix Lambert
3 Joëlle Simonet
4 Anis Maktoun
5 Hélène Frézier
6 Magali Diop

1 Angélique, France
2 Félix, Belgium
3 Joëlle, Switzerland
4 Anis, Algeria
5 Hélène, Canada
6 Magali, Senegal

p.16 Speaking

Your answers will start like this:
1 Je m'appelle …
2 J'ai … ans
3 J'habite …
4 Je suis …
5 Je parle …
6 J'apprends …

Any three of:
- Comment vous appelez-vous?
- Vous êtes de quelle nationalité?
- Où habitez-vous?
- Quelles langues parlez-vous?
- Quelles langues apprenez-vous?
- Quel âge avez-vous? (Be careful to be polite!)

p.17 Reading

1 g; **2** b; **3** h; **4** i; **5** a; **6** c; **7** d; **8** j; **9** f; **10** e

p.17 Writing

1 Je m'appelle Sophie Terrington.
2 J'ai treize ans.
3 Je suis anglaise.
4 J'habite à Norwich en Angleterre.
5 Je parle anglais et espagnol.
6 J'apprends le français.

Unit 2 Au collège

p.18 Écoutez et lisez

Le; le; le; l'; la; un

p.19 Cherchez dans le dictionnaire

la chimie – chemistry; le dessin – art, drawing; le français – French; la musique – music; le théâtre – theatre or drama

p.19 Écoutez et notez

	le ou la?	aime? ☺ n'aime pas? ☹
Exemple	le français	☺
1	la géographie	☹
2	la biologie	☺
3	les sciences	☺
4	la musique	☹
5	la technologie	☺

p.22 Lisez et répondez

1 Geography
2 Science
3 Maths
4 Music
5 Science is complicated; maths is interesting; in music you play instruments; geography is useless

p.22 Écoutez et lisez

Je suis en cinquième au collège Paul Cézanne. Le matin j'arrive au collège à huit heures et le premier cours commence à huit heures et quart. On a une récré à dix heures moins quart. Le lundi à dix heures dix j'ai maths et j'aime bien ça. Le déjeuner est à midi moins quart. Après le déjeuner on a géo. Le mardi on a les clubs sportifs après l'école. C'est nul. J'aime le mercredi parce qu'on commence plus tard et on finit à quatorze heures quinze.

p.23 Écoutez et notez

1 19.05; **2** 1.50; **3** 2.10; **4** 21.30; **5** 13.43

p.24 Vrai, faux ou on ne sait pas?

1 Vrai; **2** Vrai; **3** Faux; **4** Vrai; **5** On ne sait pas

p.27 Remplissez les blancs

Mon école s'appelle Lycée Cheikh Anta Diop. Je vais à l'école du lundi au vendredi. Le matin on nettoie les salles de classes. J'ai cours de sept heures et demie à midi. Au Sénégal on parle français et wolof. On fait de l'athlétisme. À midi on mange à la cantine. L'après-midi je travaille à la maison. Je fais mes devoirs.

p.28 J'aime lire

1 f
2 c
3 d
4 e
5 g
6 b
7 a

Practice Test Questions

p.30 Listening

	lundi
8h00–9h00	sciences
9h00–10h00	sciences
Récréation	
10h15–11h15	**géographie**
11h15–12h15	français
Déjeuner	
14h00–15h00	**histoire**
15h00–16h00	éducation civique
	club d'informatique

mardi	mercredi
français	**EPS**
français	**EPS**
Récréation	
maths	sciences
espagnol	sciences
Déjeuner	
travaux manuels	–
travaux manuels	–
club de théâtre	–

jeudi	vendredi
technologie	maths
dessin	maths
Récréation	
musique	français
anglais	espagnol
Déjeuner	
maths	**anglais**
géographie	**anglais**
clubs sportifs	

p.30 Speaking

- Salut!/Ça va?/Bonjour
- J'apprends le français.
- Le lundi j'ai/on a maths et sciences.
- Je n'aime pas l'allemand.
- Parce que le prof est sévère.

p.30 Reading

1 5
2 8.30
3 10.45
4 midday/12.00
5 14.00
6 17.00
7 1 hour
8 in the evening

p.31 Writing

1 Je déteste la musique, parce que le prof est trop sévère.
2 J'adore l'histoire parce que c'est intéressant.
3 J'adore l'EPS parce que j'aime le sport.
4 Je déteste l'espagnol parce que c'est inutile.
5 Je n'aime pas les sciences parce que le prof est ennuyeux.
6 J'aime l'anglais parce que c'est utile.
7 J'aime les travaux manuels parce que le prof est marrant.
8 J'aime le français parce que c'est facile.

Answers

Unit 3 Chez moi

p.32 Écoutez et lisez

- Tu t'entends bien avec ta <u>famille</u>, Jérémy?
- Oui et non. Je m'entends assez bien avec mes <u>parents</u>. Mais mon <u>frère</u> et ma <u>sœur</u>, quel désastre!
- Pourquoi?
- Je partage une chambre avec mon <u>frère</u> et il est têtu et égoïste. Il ne range jamais notre chambre. Et ma <u>sœur</u>, elle m'énerve. Et toi, Élodie? Vous êtes combien dans ta <u>famille</u>?
- Dans ma <u>famille</u>, nous sommes deux. Je suis <u>fille unique</u> et j'habite avec ma <u>mère</u>. Mon <u>père</u> habite avec mes <u>grands-parents</u>. Mes <u>parents</u> sont divorcés.
- Et tu t'entends bien avec ta <u>mère</u>?
- Oui, elle est gentille et drôle.

p.34 Devinez puis vérifiez

1	mon	4	mon, mes
2	ma	5	ton, Mon
3	ma, notre	6	votre, vos

p.36 Vrai ou faux?

1	Faux	4	Vrai
2	Faux	5	Vrai
3	Vrai		

p.36 Écoutez et notez

	✓/?
1	?
2	?
3	✓
4	?
5	✓

p.37 Cherchez dans le dictionnaire

1	une araignée	-s spider
2	un chat	-s cat
3	un chien	-s dog
4	un cochon d'Inde	-s guinea pig
5	un lapin	-s rabbit
6	un oiseau	-x bird
7	un poisson	-s fish
8	un serpent	-s snake
9	une souris	(no plural ending) mouse
10	une tortue	-s tortoise

p.38 Traduisez les phrases

1 I have a pet at home.
2 We have four dogs.
3 I have two mice. They are three years old.
4 She has twenty fish.
5 My little brother has seven rabbits.

p.40 Remplissez les blancs

1	sur	5	entre
2	sous	6	dans
3	à côté de	7	derrière
4	sur		

p.42 Reliez les phrases

1 d; 2 e; 3 b; 4 a; 5 c

p.43 J'aime lire!

actress; animals; farm; vegetarian; Foundation; Protection; Domestic; visit; captivity; experimentation; moment; massacre; Canadian Government; furious

Practice Test Questions

p.45 Listening

	😊	☹
Exemple	sister	brother
1	mother	father
2	uncle	aunt
3	grandparents	
4		twin sisters
5		brother
6		dog

p.45 Speaking

Sample answers
1 Nous sommes (2/3/4/5) dans ma famille.
2 Oui, j'ai (un chat/une tortue)/Non, je n'ai pas d'animal.
3 Oui, je partage ma chambre avec (ma sœur/mon frère)/Non, je ne partage pas ma chambre.
4 Oui, j'ai (un frère/une sœur/deux frères/deux sœurs)/Non, je suis fils/fille unique.
5 Oui, j'aide à la maison, par exemple je …/ Non, je n'aide pas à la maison.
6 Oui, je m'entends bien avec ma mère/Non, je me n'entends pas bien avec ma mère.

p.45 Reading

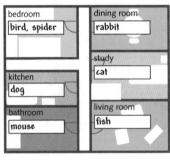

p.46 Writing

1 Je range ma chambre. **OR** Je ne range pas ma chambre.
2 Je fais la vaisselle. **OR** Je ne fais pas la vaisselle.
3 Je fais les lits. **OR** Je ne fais pas les lits.
4 Je fais les courses. **OR** Je ne fais pas les courses.
5 Je fais la cuisine. **OR** Je ne fais pas la cuisine.
6 Je lave la voiture. **OR** Je ne lave pas la voiture.
7 Je travaille dans le jardin. **OR** Je ne travaille pas dans le jardin.

Unit 4 Comment tu t'amuses?

p.47 Écoutez et lisez

The boy is trying to invite the girl to go to the cinema. The film is a horror comedy adapted from a romantic detective novel. The girl thinks this sounds awful and tries to think of an excuse, so says she has to go to the dentist. When the boy is surprised that she's going to the dentist on a Saturday evening, she says it's a special offer!

p.48 Écoutez et notez

1 un dessin animé, et son chien
2 un film pour enfants, livre pour enfants
3 un film d'aventure fantastique, livre très long
4 un film pour enfants, quatre enfants
5 une comédie romantique, famille de douze enfants
6 une comédie de science-fiction, anglais, livre

p.50 Traduisez en anglais

1 At the weekends he does weight training.
2 She does sport at school.
3 On Saturdays they go climbing.
4 On Wednesdays after school, they go riding.
5 In Winter people/they/we go skiing.
6 I love going cycling!

p.51 Écoutez et notez

1	computer	4	drums
2	video games	5	piano
3	football	6	keyboard

p.53 Écoutez et notez

	Free time
1	likes collecting toys
2	loves collecting stickers
3	likes doing homework
4	loves swimming
5	likes surfing the web

p.54 Écoutez et notez

Tu veux …?		Je ne peux pas. Je dois …	
aller au cinéma	1	aller chez le dentiste	1
aller faire les magasins	5	aller chez ma grand-mère	
aller dans un café		faire du babysitting	3
aller au concert	2	faire les courses	7
aller en ville		faire mes devoirs	4
aller au parc	6	laver mon chien	2
sortir samedi soir	7	me laver les cheveux	6
venir à la fête foraine	3	promener mon chien	
venir à une soirée		ranger mon tiroir à chaussettes	
venir avec moi	4	rester à la maison	5

p.54 Écrivez des phrases

- Tu veux aller dans un café?
- Je ne peux pas. Je dois aller chez ma grand-mère.

- Tu veux aller en ville?
- Je ne peux pas. Je dois promener mon chien.

- Tu veux venir à une soirée?
- Je ne peux pas. Je dois ranger mon tiroir à chaussettes.

p.55 J'aime lire!

1 Le monde de Narnia
2 Wallace et Gromit, le mystère du lapin-garou
3 Charlie et la chocolaterie

these children – ces enfants
this factory – cette fabrique
this film – ce film
this magic world – ce monde magique
this man – cet homme
this wardrobe – cette armoire

Practice Test Questions

p.57 Listening

lundi 17 dentist	vendredi 21 skating in Paris
mardi 18 climbing	samedi 22 cricket
mercredi 19 skiing	dimanche 23 stay at home and do homework
jeudi 20 chess competition	

p.57 Reading

The film has been adapted from a children's book.
It is a cartoon.
The story is about a strange family.
The family lives in a very large, magic house.
The daughter rides her bike on her bed.
The son wants to play football all the time, even in the bathroom!
The dog plays in an orchestra.
The grandmother babysits but she is a spider.
The mother skates in the sock drawer.
There is a funfair in the kitchen.
But there is also a mystery – who is living in the wardrobe?

p.58 Speaking

– Qu'est-ce que tu fais de ton temps libre?
– **Je joue d'un instrument/de la guitare/du piano etc.**
– Tu aimes faire du sport?
– **Je fais du judo et de la natation.**
– Tu veux aller au cinéma ce week-end?
– **Qu'est-ce que c'est comme film?**
– C'est un film policier adapté d'un livre.
– **Je dois faire mes devoirs.**

p.58 Writing

1 En hiver, je fais du ski.
2 Au printemps, je fais du vélo.
3 En automne, je fais de la musculation.
4 En été, je fais de la natation.
5 En automne, je fais du skate.
6 En hiver, je fais de la danse.
7 Au printemps, je vais au parc.
8 En été, je promène le chien.
9 En hiver, je vais au concert.
10 En été, j'aime lire.

Unit 5 Vacances en France

p.60 Recopiez avec la bonne phrase

1 Thomas est belge.
2 Thomas n'aime pas rendre visite à sa grand-mère.
3 Il n'aime pas les vacances de Pâques.
4 En été il passe deux semaines en France.
5 Il aime faire de la natation.
6 Il préférait dormir dans une tente.

p.61 Écoutez et soulignez

Qu'est-ce qu'il y a à faire à Carcassonne?
Carcassonne est une ville très pittoresque. Il y a la vieille ville, où on peut visiter le château. Il y a des petites rues, où on peut prendre le déjeuner dans un café. Il y a beaucoup à voir, par exemple, la cathédrale et des musées. On peut faire des promenades dans la vieille ville. Il y a le Canal du Midi, où on peut faire des promenades en bateau. Il y a aussi la ville moderne où on peut aller à la piscine ou au théâtre.

p.62 Regardez et décidez

e, b, j, l, g, d

p.63 Traduisez en anglais

1 They ignore their teachers.
2 They buy souvenirs.
3 They do (are doing) their homework.
4 They take part in (belong to) a gym club.
5 They think (are thinking) about their holidays.
6 They go for boat trips on the Canal du Midi.

p.64 Écoutez et soulignez

L'année dernière j'ai passé mes vacances en France. J'ai dormi dans un hôtel à Carcassonne avec mes parents. Nous avons visité la vieille ville et quelques musées. J'ai nagé dans la piscine chaque jour. Ma mère a acheté beaucoup de vêtements. Chaque soir nous avons mangé dans un restaurant différent. J'ai beaucoup aimé Carcassonne.

p.66 Complétez les phrases

1 J'ai pris mon petit déjeuner dans un café.
2 J'ai voyagé en Eurostar.
3 J'ai fait une excursion en bateau sur le Canal du Midi.
4 J'ai acheté un t-shirt comme souvenir.
5 J'ai lu un livre intéressant.
6 J'ai mangé une grande glace au chocolat.
7 J'ai regardé un film à la télé.
8 J'ai écouté de la musique rock pendant le voyage.

p.66 Écoutez et lisez

Disliked: Oliver, the weather in England; staying at Oliver's house, sharing a room with Oliver, Oliver not going to London

p.68 Remplissez les blancs

1 Il est né en France.
2 Elles sont allées en Angleterre.
3 Vous êtes arrivés à quelle heure?
4 Elle est partie à huit heures.
5 Ils sont tombés du vélo.
6 Nous sommes montés dans la tour Eiffel.

p.69 J'aime lire!

1 la destination la plus populaire pour les touristes
2 les français passent leurs vacances en France
3 des vins connus
4 une maison secondaire à la campagne
5 pour profiter du bon climat
6 on va à la montagne

Practice Test Questions

p.70 Listening

a 1; b 2; c 7; d 3; e 9; f 5; g 4; h 6; i 8; j 10

p.70 Speaking

– Où est-ce que tu vas pendant les vacances?
– **Normalement, je rends (on rend) visite à mes grands-parents.**
– Où es-tu allé(e) l'année dernière en vacances?
– **L'année dernière je suis allé(e) (on est allé) en France.**
– Qu'est-ce que tu as fait?
– **J'ai (On a) visité des musées et des châteaux.**
– Où est-ce que tu as mangé?
– **J'ai (On a) mangé dans des restaurants français.**
– Tu aimes la France?
– **Oui, je me suis bien amusé(e).**

p.71 Reading

1 e; 2 d; 3 g; 4 f; 5 b; 6 a; 7 c

p.71 Writing

On peut aller au café.
On peut visiter le musée.
On peut aller à la piscine.
On peut faire des promenades à vélo.
On peut visiter le château.
On peut faire des promenades en bateau.

Unit 6 Mon look

p.72 Écoutez et lisez

Je préfère un look décontracté, par exemple un pantalon pattes d'éléphants et une chemise. J'aime les couleurs sombres. C'est un style branché.

J'aime le look sport. Je mets un sweat et un pantalon de jogging chaque jour. Mon look est pratique et confortable. Tous mes vêtements sont de la marque de mon équipe de foot, les Bleus. Et ma couleur préférée, c'est bien sûr le bleu!

J'aime le look habillé parce que c'est chic et élégant. Je me maquille chaque jour et je m'occupe de ma coiffure. Quand je m'habille, je pense beaucoup aux couleurs qui me vont. Je préfère les couleurs noir et blanc parce qu'elles sont super à la mode!

Mon look? Je porte un jean et un sweat. S'il fait chaud, je porte un tee-shirt et un short. Voilà mon look. Les vêtements et la mode et tout ça, ça ne m'intéressent pas.

p.73 Regardez et décidez

Description b.

p.75 Écoutez et notez

	Looking for …	Buys it? ✓ / X
1	skirt, black leather, short	✓
2	woollen pullover, yellow, medium	X
3	black cotton trainers, size 52	X
4	souvenir tee-shirt of Paris, small, beige	✓

p.78 C'est logique!

	Yeux				Cheveux			
	bleus	bruns	noirs	verts	blonds	bruns	noirs	roux
André	X	X	X	✓	X	X	X	✓
Benoît	X	X	✓	X	✓	X	X	X
Céline	✓	X	X	X	X	X	✓	X
Didi	X	✓	X	X	X	✓	X	X

	Look			
	décontracté	habillé	pas de sport	sport
André	✓	X	X	X
Benoît	X	✓	X	X
Céline	X	X	X	✓
Didi	X	X	✓	X

p.79 Écoutez et lisez

Je me réveille à sept heures et je me lève à sept heures et quart. D'abord, je me lave, puis je m'habille. Je prends mon petit déjeuner et après je me brosse les dents. Je pars à l'école à huit heures moins le quart. Je rentre à la maison à quatre heures et demie et je prends mon goûter tout de suite. Je me couche à dix heures.

p.80 Écoutez et notez

1 Je me réveille /~~me lève~~ à sept heures.
2 Il se couche/~~se brosse les dents~~ à onze heures.
3 Elles ~~s'occupent de~~/s'intéressent à leurs vêtements.
4 Je ~~me lave~~/me brosse les cheveux.
5 On s'amuse/~~se lave~~ bien.
6 Elle s'entend bien avec/~~s'occupe de~~ sa sœur.

p.81 Écoutez et lisez

on ne porte pas; trouvent; on porte; C'est

p.82 Lisez et trouvez les verbes

1 j'étais
2 j'allais
3 Je portais
4 j'adorais
5 On portait
6 étaient
7 lavait
8 je voulais
9 j'avais

p.83 J'aime lire!

Dear white brother,
When I was born, I was black
When I grew up, I was black
When I go out in the sun, I am black
When I am afraid, I am black
When I am ill, I am black
Whereas, you, white man
When you were born, you were pink,
When you grew up, you were white,
When you go out in the sun, you are red,
When you are cold, you are blue,
When you are frightened, you are green,
When you are ill, you are yellow,
And after that, you dare to call me a 'man of colour'?

Practice Test Questions

p.85 Listening

Tania   Sophie   Émilie   Mélissa

p.85 Speaking

Bonjour, vous désirez?
Je voudrais une veste en cuir.
De quelle couleur?
Brune, s'il vous plaît.
De quelle taille?
De taille moyenne, s'il vous plaît.
Voilà une veste très chic. C'est trois cents euros.
C'est trop cher. Ça ne me va pas.
Voilà une veste plus décontractée. C'est cent euros.
Je l'aime. Je la prends.
Voilà, je vous en prie.
Merci. Au revoir.

p.86 Reading

Africa is **black** like my skin
It is red like the earth.
It is white like the midday light.
It is blue like the evening shade.
It is yellow like the big river.
It is green like the palm leaf.
Africa has all the colours of life.

p.86 Writing

1 Elle se douche.
2 Elle s'habille/Elle met ses vêtements/Elle porte un tee-shirt blanc et un pullover rouge
3 Elle s'occupe de ses cheveux/Elle a les cheveux bruns/mi-longs
4 Elle porte/met des lunettes.
5 Elle prend son petit déjeuner.
6 Elle se brosse les dents.
7 Elle part à huit heures moins le quart/sept heures quarante-cinq.

Unit 7 Métro et météo

p.87 Écoutez et complétez le plan

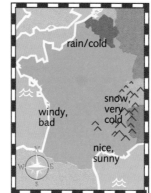

p.89 Regardez et complétez

1 Dans le sud de la France, sur la côte méditerranéenne, il faisait/il y avait du brouillard.
2 À la montagne, dans les Alpes, il neigeait.
3 Dans l'ouest de la France, il faisait/il y avait du vent.
4 À Paris, il pleuvait.
5 Au nord-est de la France, il faisait chaud/du soleil.

p.91 Imaginez le voyage

a 6; b 1; c 9; d 8; e 7; f 5; g 4; h 2; i 3

p.92 Écoutez et lisez

J'habite à Sochaux. C'est une ville <u>industrielle</u> dans la région Franche–Comté à 440 kilomètres de Paris. C'est un peu <u>sale</u>. Dans ma ville il y a un centre commercial. Je n'aime pas beaucoup ma ville parce que c'est <u>ennuyeux</u> et trop loin de la mer.

La <u>meilleure</u> chose dans ma ville, c'est que les gens sont <u>sympas</u>.

La <u>pire</u> chose dans ma ville, c'est la pollution.

p.93 Décrivez votre région

Sample Answer

J'habite à Hull.

C'est dans la région East Yorkshire à 70 kilomètres de York.

C'est une ville historique mais un peu ennuyeuse.

Dans ma ville il y a un grand centre commercial, qui s'appelle Princes Quay.

J'aime ma ville, parce que les gens sont sympas.

La meilleure chose dans ma ville, c'est l'aquarium moderne, qui s'appelle 'The Deep'.

La pire chose dans ma ville, c'est le climat parce qu'il fait toujours froid.

p.95 Écoutez et notez

3, 5, 4, 1, 2

p.95 J'aime lire!

1 1900
2 Paris
3 Line 1/the first line
4 Because this style was fashionable at the time the first metro stations were built.
5 Line 4
6 To make the ride more comfortable
7 No
8 It is used in the rest of the world to describe underground railways.

Practice Test Questions

p.97 Listening

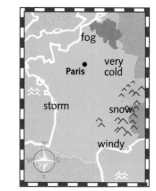

p.97 Speaking

1 Quand il pleut, je prends le bus.
2 Quand il fait froid, je reste à la maison.
3 Quand il neige, je fais du ski.
4 Quand il fait du soleil, je fais les magasins.
5 Quand il fait chaud, je vais à la plage.

p.98 Reading

1 b; 2 a; 3 d; 4 e; 5 c

p.98 Writing

J'habite à Carcassonne.
C'est dans la région Languedoc-Roussillon.
C'est à cent kilomètres de Toulouse.
C'est pittoresque et historique.
Dans ma ville il y a un grand château et la vieille ville.
J'aime ma ville, parce que c'est intéressant.
La pire chose dans ma ville, c'est qu'il y a un trop de touristes.

Unit 8 La santé

p.99 Écoutez et lisez

tu as = 5; j'ai = 5; je n'ai pas = 1

p.100 Cherchez dans le dictionnaire

la bouche(s) – mouth
le corps(-) – body
le cou(s) – neck
la dent(s) – tooth
le doigt(s) – finger
le dos(-) – back
le genou(x) – knee
la gorge(s) – throat
le nez(-) – nose

p.102 Écoutez et notez

1	headache, arms hurt, feels cold, thinks he has flu
2	feels ill, stomach ache and wants to vomit
3	feels sleepy, legs hurt, back aches
4	feels hot, thirsty, feet hurt and very tired

p.103 Devinez et écoutez

The pharmacist advises Katie: use cream (10), take some aspirin (3), stay in bed (12), drink lots of water (9), avoid the sun (8).

p.103 Écoutez et lisez

Does sport quite often; goes to the swimming pool twice a week; eats fruit and vegetables four or five times a day; avoids cola usually; eats junk food sometimes; refuses cigarettes always; goes to bed later at weekends; has too much homework every day.

p.105 Completez les phrases

Many answers are possible here.

p.105 Lisez et répondez

Healthy person's answers: **1** a; **2** b; **3** c; **4** c; **5** a
Unhealthy person's answers: **1** b; **2** a; **3** a; **4** a; **5** c

p.107 Trouvez la traduction

1 c; **2** e; **3** a; **4** b; **5** d; **6** g; **7** f

p.107 J'aime lire!

1 b; **2** d; **3** a; **4** c; **5** e; **6** g; **7** f

Practice Test Questions

p.109 Listening

	Problem	Advice
1	Eyes hurt	Go to doctor's (immediately)
2	Feet hurt	Use cream
3	Leg hurts	Go to the hospital
4	Toothache	Go to the dentist (of course)
5	Flu	Stay in bed
6	Headache	Take some tablets
7	Stomach ache	Drink lots of water and eat some yogurt
8	Hand hurts	Use a plaster
9	Wants to vomit	Don't eat
10	Can't sleep	Avoid coffee and take this prescription

p.109 Speaking

Bonjour. Qu'est-ce que tu as?
J'ai mal à la tête.
Tu as chaud?
J'ai soif.
Tu étais au soleil hier?
Je suis allé(e) à la plage.
Tu as un coup de soleil.
Qu'est-ce qu'il faut faire?
Reste à la maison et bois beaucoup d'eau.
Merci. Au revoir.

p.110 Reading

1	✓	6	✓
2	X	7	X
3	✓	8	X
4	X	9	X
5	X	10	✓

p.110 Writing

You could start each sentence with: je vais, je dois, je veux, il faut, on peut, il vaut mieux
1 … faire plus de sport.
2 … refuser les cigarettes/le tabac.
3 … me coucher tôt.
4 … manger des fruits chaque jour.
5 … éviter le stress.
6 … aller au collège à pied.
7 … boire moins de coca.
8 … manger plus de légumes.
9 … aller en ville à vélo.
10 … faire de la natation/aller à la piscine/nager deux fois par semaine.

Unit 9 Guide pratique

p.111 Écoutez et lisez

– Bonjour. Vous désirez?
– Avez-vous du jambon, s'il vous plaît?
– Bien sûr. Combien vous en voulez?
– Alors, je voudrais <u>quatre</u> tranches de jambon.
– C'est tout?
– Non, c'est combien le pâté?
– <u>Dix-sept</u> euros le kilo.
– J'en prends <u>cinq cents</u> grammes.
– Voilà. Encore quelque chose?
– Oui. Qu'est-ce que vous avez comme plats préparés?
– Nous avons des quiches, de la salade et du

saucisson sec.
– J'en veux un assortiment, s'il vous plaît. Et c'est tout.
– Ça fait <u>quarante-deux</u> euros, s'il vous plaît.

p.113 C'est quelle quantité?

100g de/un morceau de fromage
un litre de lait
une bouteille de/un litre de vin rouge
un paquet de chips
une (deux) tranche(s) de/100g de jambon
un kilo de/100g de tomates
une portion de/100g de salade préparée
une portion de quiche
un pot de moutarde
une boîte de thon

p.114 Écoutez et lisez

The customers are making life difficult for the waiter, so when they ask him what he recommends, he recommends the restaurant next door!

p.115 Écrivez des phrases

1 Il ne mange pas de viande parce qu'il est végétarien.
2 Elle ne mange pas de sucre parce qu'elle est diabétique.
3 Il ne mange pas de blé parce qu'il est allergique.
4 On ne mange pas de porc parce qu'on est juif.
5 Je ne mange pas de cacahouètes.

p.115 Recopiez les plats dans la carte

Hors d'œuvres
Crudités   Salade de tomates
Soupe du jour

Plats principaux
Bifteck   Côtelette d'agneau
Omelette au choix   Poisson du jour
Rôti de porc

Desserts
Compote de fruits   Mélange de glaces
Mousse au chocolat   Tarte aux pommes

Casse-croûtes
Crêpe au fromage   Croque-monsieur
Sandwich au pâté

Boissons
Carafe de rouge   Citron pressé
Eau   Jus de fruit

p.117 Écoutez et notez

	Where to?	Ticket?
1	Paris	return, second class
2	Lille	single, non-smoking
3	Nîmes	first class
4	Biarritz	single for the next train
5	Lyon	first class return
6	La Rochelle	the next train

p.119 Vrai ou faux?

Faux (you take the first left, not the first right at the end).

p.120 Écoutez et notez

	C'est qui?
1	Éric
2	Clément
3	Fouzia
4	Denis
5	Annick
6	Barbara

p.121 J'aime lire!

There are three pyramids at the Louvre, but only two are made of glass.

Practice Test Questions

122 Listening

100g – prepared salad   1 litre – white wine
250g – cheese   a bottle – milk
500g – salami   a piece – quiche
1kg – tomatoes   a slice – ham

p.122 Speaking

Sample answers:
1 Je voudrais envoyer deux cartes postales au pays de Galles. C'est combien?
2 Une télécarte à vingt euro s'il vous plaît.
3 Je voudrais trois timbres à un euro, s'il vous plaît.
4 Une télécarte à dix euro, s'il vous plaît.
5 Je voudrais envoyer une carte postale en Angleterre, s'il vous plaît.
6 Je voudrais envoyer une lettre en Angleterre, s'il vous plaît.
7 Je voudrais deux timbres à soixante cents, s'il vous plaît.
8 Où est la boîte aux lettres, s'il vous plaît?
9 Je voudrais envoyer une lettre au pays de Galles, s'il vous plaît.
10 Je voudrais envoyer un colis en Écosse.

p.123 Reading

1 e; **2** b; **3** a; **4** c; **5** f; **6** d
1 4th; **2** 2nd; **3** 3rd; **4** 1st; **5** 5th;
6 10th; **7** 1st; **8** 18th; **9** 2nd; **10** 8th

p.123 Writing

Allez tout droit. Prenez la première rue à droite. Prenez la première rue à gauche/Tournez à gauche. Continuez tout droit. Prenez la première rue à gauche. Le parc est à gauche.

Unit 10 J'adore la techno

p.124 Écoutez et notez

	favourite programme	hours of TV per day	extra
1	music	3–4	favourite channel = M6
2	game shows	at least 4	watches too much TV
3	series/soaps	all the time	has TV in bedroom and watches even while doing homework or on phone
4	sport	1–2	hates reality TV
5	films on DVD	never	prefers surfing the Internet
6	American films	2–3	finds news and weather boring

p.126 Devinez puis écoutez

1 J'étais au ciné(ma)
2 À demain
3 C'est bien
4 C'est pas sympa
5 J'ai une idée
6 J'ai acheté un cadeau
7 Quoi de neuf?
8 J'étais énervé
9 J'étais occupé
10 Je sais
11 Merci
12 rien de neuf

p.127 Écoutez et notez

1 Je suis allé avec mes amis.
2 Il est son petit ami depuis un an.
3 J'ai plus ou moins le même âge.
4 Comment allez-vous?
5 Vous avez deux enfants?
6 David aime les escargots.
7 Nous en avons beaucoup.
8 Il n'y a rien à manger.

p.129 Lisez et notez

Olivier is asking Mireille out.
Sabrina is breaking up with Ahmed.
Marie-Noëlle is ill.
Liliane is in love with Jacques.
Zoë is on holiday.
Saïd is thanking Danielle for a present.
Gérard Andine is turning down an invitation from Madame Dubois.
Madame de Villepin is writing an absence note for her son, Hervé.

p.131 Trouvez dans le dictionnaire

	conventional meaning	meaning in technology
accueil (m)	welcome	homepage
le bouton	spot	button
chercher	to look for	search
fermer cette fenêtre	to close this window	close this window
un lien	link	hyperlink
la recherche	research	search
retour à la page précédente	return to the previous page	backward
suite	following	forward

p.132 Lisez et notez

1 DD
2 TT
3 MM
4 TT
5 MM
6 DD
7 TT
8 DD

p.134 J'aime lire!

La publicité à la télé

Les plus grandes marques dépensent beaucoup d'argent pour faire de la publicité à la télé. On dit que la pub paie les émissions de bonne qualité. Mais qui paie la pub? Toi et moi, quand nous achetons ces produits!

Les pubs les plus connues sont aussi populaires que les émissions. Quelques téléfans préfèrent la pub aux émissions, parce qu'elles sont amusantes et mémorables.

La pub a une influence énorme. Par exemple, la musique de Moby et l' acteur Anthony Head sont devenus connus par la pub.

Les jeunes sont influencés par la publicité. La pub encourage les jeunes à acheter un produit. Dans quelques pays, la pub pour les enfants est interdite.

Les enfants très jeunes sont les plus impressionnants. Ils ne comprennent pas que la pub est là pour vendre des produits. Ils pensent que c'est encore leur émission préferée.

Trouvez l'intrus
• In some countries the adverts last almost as long as the TV programmes.

Practice Test Questions

p.136 Listening

1 ☺; 2 ☹; 3 ☺; 4 ☺; 5 ☹; 6 ☺; 7 ☺; 8 ☺; 9 ☹

p.136 Speaking

1 J'aime les émissions sportives et musicales.
2 Je n'aime pas les infos et la météo.
3 Ma chaîne préférée est Channel 4.
4 Je regarde la télé quatre heures par jour.
5 Je regarde Friends et Coronation Street.

p.137 Reading

1 home page
2 search
3 click here
4 close this window
5 useful links
6 the results of your search
7 return (to previous page)
8 next (page)

p.137 Writing

Besançon, le 24 mai

Chère Margrite,

J'ai un problème. J'ai des boutons. Je voudrais acheter une crème antiseptique. Mais mes parents ne sont pas d'accord. Pourquoi??? J'en ai besoin pour mes boutons. Malheureusement, je n'ai pas d'argent de poche. Je ne sais pas quoi faire.
Aidez-moi!

Le Boutonneux de Besançon

Unit 11 Le petit boulot

p.139 Écoutez et notez

	How much?	Who gives it?	Spends it on?	Saving?
1	20 euro	parents	video games and music	no
2	20 euro	granddad and mother (10 euro each)	mobile phone calls	new mobile
3	15 euro	parents	sport and magazines	new bike
4	45 euro	no one/ has a job	going out	–

p.142 Écoutez et vérifiez

1 Où
2 quelle
3 comment
4 combien
5 Coment
6 Qu'
7 Quand
8 combien
9 Pourquoi

p.144 Ecoutez et lisez

1 Élodie
2 Matthieu
3 Yannick
4 Mélanie
5 Arnaud
6 Matthieu
7 Arnaud
8 Yannick
9 Mélanie
10 Arnaud

p.146 Trouvez le numéro secret

1 1, 11, 14; 2 1, 15, 16; 3 22, 24, 25;
4 1, 15, 17, 2, 8; 5 23, 1, 11, 13

p.148 Traduisez en français

1 J'apprends à manger plus sainment.
2 J'ai décidé de devenir végétarien(ne).
3 J'essaie de faire mes devoirs.
4 Je refuse de fumer des cigarettes.
5 J'ai arrêté de boire du coca.
6 Je commence à nager.

p.149 J'aime lire!

b, c, g, i are not mentioned in the text.

Practice Test Questions

p.150 Listening

1 b; 2 c; 3 a; 4 c; 5 a; 6 c; 7 c; 8 a; 9 a; 10 c

p.151 Speaking

1 Je reçois 10 livres par semaine.
2 Mes grands-parents me donnent mon argent de poche.
3 Je fais du jardinage/Je travaille dans le jardin.
4 Je dépense mon argent en … /J'achète … DVDs et magazines/Je paie mes appels sur mon portable.
5 Je fais des économies pour acheter un portable/un vélo.

p.151 Reading

1 b; 2 h; 3 d; 4 i; 5 a; 6 e; 7 j; 8 g; 9 c; 10 f;

p.151 Writing

1 J'apprends à nager.
2 Je continue à manger plus sainement.
3 J'ai décidé de chercher un petit boulot.
4 Je refuse de fumer (des cigarettes).
5 J'ai arrêté de boire du coca.
6 Je commence à faire mes devoirs.
7 J'essaie de devenir végétarien(ne).
8 J'ai décidé de devenir professeur.
9 J'essaie de manger moins de chocolat.
10 Je continue à faire plus de sport.

Unit 12 Le monde francophone

p.152 Écoutez et lisez

Environ cent soixante millions de gens dans le monde parlent français. On parle français comme langue maternelle ou langue officielle dans quarante-quatre pays et sur quatre continents. En Europe, une partie des Belges et des Suisses parle français. En Amerique du Nord on parle français en Louisiane et au Canada. En Amerique du Sud on parle français aux Antilles et au Haïti. En Afrique on parle français dans une vingtaine de pays. Même en Asie, on parle français en Laos, Cambodge et au Viêt-nam. Dans autres pays, le nombre de gens qui apprennent le français a augmenté plus de vingt pour cent dans les dix dernières années.

p.153 Écoutez et notez

Belgique – .be
Burkina Faso – .bf
Cambodge – .kh
Cameroun – .cm
Canada – .ca
Congo – .cg
Côte d'Ivoire – .ci
France – .fr
Laos – .la
Luxembourg – .lu
Mali – .ml
Madagascar – .mg
Sénégal – .sn
Tchad – .td
Tunisie – .tn

p.154 Écoutez et vérifiez

le 1er janvier	le jour de l'An
le 14 février	la Saint Valentin
le 1er avril	poisson d'avril
le 1er mai	la fête du travail
le 14 juillet	la fête nationale
août	vacances!
la première semaine de septembre	la rentrée des classes
le 31 octobre	Halloween
le 31 décembre	La Saint-Sylvestre/le réveillon

p.157 Vrai, faux ou on ne sait pas?

	✓/X/?
Exemple	?
1	✓
2	X
3	✓
4	?
5	✓
6	✓
7	X
8	X

p.158 Écoutez et notez

1 e
2 a
3 f
4 d
5 b
6 g
7 c

p.159 Écoutez et lisez

Normalement pour célébrer mon anniversaire je vais dans un restaurant avec ma famille. Ma famille m'offre beaucoup de cadeaux et on mange bien. Mais cette année je voulais célébrer avec mes amis. J'ai organisé une petite fête pour vingt amis. J'ai acheté les chips et les boissons, j'ai choisi la musique et j'ai rangé la maison après la soirée. Je me suis bien amusée mais c'était beaucoup de travail. L'année prochaine je voudrais faire moins d'effort et je vais aller dans un resturant encore!

p.160 Remplissez les blancs

Infinitive	Perfect tense	Present tense	Future
acheter	j'ai acheté	j'achète	je vais acheter
manger	j'ai mangé	je mange	je vais manger
écouter	j'ai écouté	j'écoute	je vais écouter
parler	j'ai parlé	je parle	je vais parler
faire	j'ai fait	je fais	je vais faire
aller	je suis allé(e)	je vais	je vais aller
s'amuser	je me suis amusé(e)	je m'amuse	je vais m'amuser

p.160 J'aime lire!

Country	Senegal
Capital	Dakar
Location	West Africa, Atlantic coast
Climate	tropical, fairly hot
Exports	peanuts, fish, music
Population	12 million
Languages	French, Wolof, African languages
Religion	Muslim majority
Events	4th April – Independence Day, Muslim festivals, New Year, Paris–Dakar Rally

Practice Test Questions

p.162 Listening

	When	Activity
1	last week	swimming (pool)
2	this evening	talk to friends
3	now	eat no more meat
4	this year	learn Spanish
5	last year	had fun at the fair
6	already	did homework
7	yesterday	ate too much chocolate
8	next year	gap year
9	tomorrow morning	DVD player
10	in the future	work in a hospital

p.162 Speaking

1 Joyeux Anniversaire!
2 Joyeux Noël!
3 Bonne chance!
4 Bon voyage!
5 Bonne année!
6 Bonne journée!

p.162 Reading

People in France celebrate the Epiphany on **6 January**. People **eat** a special cake which contains a **hidden** charm. The person who finds the charm is king or queen **for the day**.

Candlemas takes place **forty days after** Christmas. **According** to tradition, people **make pancakes**.

Martinique	
Capital	Fort-de-France
Location	Caribbean
Climate	tropical
Exports	bananas, sugar, coffee
Population	400,000 (four hundred thousand)
Languages	French and Creole Patois
Religion	Catholic
Events	French national holiday, 14 July, Carnival

p.163 Writing

1 Le 25 décembre, c'est le jour de Noël.
2 C'est une fête importante en Grande-Bretagne.
3 Dans ma famille on s'amuse bien.
4 On offre des cadeaux.
5 Le soir on allume des bougies.
6 On décore un sapin de Noël.
7 Normalement, il n'y a pas de feux d'artifices.

Glossary

adj = adjective	
adv = adverb	

m = masculine	
f = feminine	

pl = plural	
prep = preposition	

à/au/aux (prep)	at, to
à la mode	in fashion
à mon avis	in my opinion
à part de	apart from
d'abord (adv)	first, at first
accent (m)	accent
d'accord	OK
acheter	to buy
à l'âge de	at the age of
aider	to help
aigu (adj)	acute
aimer	to like
Allemagne (f)	Germany
allemand (adj)	German
aller	to go
alors (adv)	in that case, so
ami (m) amie (f)	friend
amusant (adj)	amusing, funny
s'amuser	to enjoy oneself, to have a good time
an (m), année (f)	year
anniversaire (f)	birthday
appeler	to call
s'appeler	to be called
apprendre	to learn
après (prep)	after
après-midi (m)	afternoon
assez (adv)	quite
attendre	to wait for
aujourd'hui (adv)	today
aussi (adv)	also, too, as well
autre (adj)	other, further
(en) automne (m)	(in) autumn
avant (prep)	before, in front of
avec (prep)	with
à l'avenir (m)	in future
avoir	to have
beau/belle (adj)	good-looking, nice
beaucoup (adv)	a lot, much
ben	well, err
bien (adv)	good, well
bien sûr	of course
bientôt (adv)	soon

bœuf (m)	beef
bof	just about OK, so what
boire	to drink
au bord de la mer	by the sea
boucles d'oreille (f pl)	earrings
branché (adj)	up to date
breton (m/adj)	language spoken in Brittany
bûche (f)	log
ça	that
ça dépend	that depends
ça va, ça va?	OK, how are you?
ce/cet/cette (demonstrative adjective)	this
cédille (f)	cedilla
ces (demonstrative adjective)	these
c'est	it is
c'était	it was
chaque (adj)	every, each
chez (prep)	to/at the house of (**or** to/at the office of)
choisir	to choose
circonflexe (adj)	circumflex
circulation (f)	traffic
collège (m)	secondary school
combien (adv)	how much, how many
comme (adv)	as, like
commencer	to begin
comment (adv)	how
comprendre	to understand
concours (m)	competition
contre (prep)	against
courrier électronique (m), courriel (m)	email
copain (m)	(boy)friend
copine (f)	(girl)friend
cours (m)	lesson, course
courses (f pl)	shopping
court (adj)	short
côte (f)	coast

à côté de	beside, next to
cuisine (f)	kitchen, cooking
d'abord (adv)	first, at first
d'accord	OK
dans (prep)	in
de (prep)	of, from
de temps en temps	from time to time
déjà (adv)	already
demain (adv)	tomorrow
demander	to ask (for)
demi/e (adj)	half
depuis (prep)	since
dernier(ière) (adj)	last
derrière (prep)	behind
deuxième (adj)	second
devant (prep)	in front of
devenir	to become
devoir	to have to, 'must', 'ought'
devoirs (m pl)	homework
digramme (m)	digraph, two letters joined to make new sound, usually œ
dire	to say
divers (adj)	varied, diverse
donc (conjunction)	so, therefore, consequently
donner	to give
dossier (m)	file. folder
école (f) (primaire/ maternelle)	school (primary/ nursery school)
écossais (adj), Écosse (f)	Scottish, Scotland
écouter	to listen
écrire	to write
éléphant (m)	elephant
élève (m or f)	pupil
elle (personal pronoun)	she
elles (personal pronoun)	they
en (prep or pronoun)	in, to, of that
en fait	in fact
en général	in general
en plus	moreover/besides

en tout cas	in any case	habiter	to live	le meilleur/ la meilleure/ les meilleurs	the best
encore (adv)	still, yet, again	d'habitude (adv)	usually		
énerver	to annoy	heure (f)	hour, o'clock	même (adj/adv)	same, even
ensuite (adv)	next, then, afterwards	hier (adv)	yesterday	mer (f)	sea
		(en) hiver (m)	(in) winter	mettre	to put, to put on
entendre	to hear	histoire (f)	story, history	mieux	better
s'entendre avec	to get on with	hôtel (m)	hotel	mince (adj)	thin, slim
entre (prep)	between	ici (adv)	here	minimessage (m)	text message
entrée (f)	starter, entrance	il (personal pronoun)	he	minuit (m)	midnight
environ (adv)	about, round			moi (pronoun)	me
envoyer	to send	ils (personal pronoun)	they	le moins	the least
est (m)	east (also see être, page 33)	il y a	there is, there are	moins ... que	less ... than
		il y avait	there was, there were	mon/ma/mes (possessive adj)	my
est-ce que ... ?	is ...? (used to begin a question)				
		île (f)	isle, island	monde (m)	world
essayer	to try	jamais (adv)	never	monter	to climb
et (conjunction)	and	je (personal pronoun)	I	nager	to swim
été (m)	summer			naissance (f)	birth
être	to be	jouer	to play	naïf/naïve (adj)	naïve, ingenuous
éviter	to avoid	journal (m)	newspaper, diary	naturellement (adv)	naturally, of course
faire	to do, to make	jour (m)/journée (f)	day	nettoyer	to clean
il faut	you have to	jusqu'à (prep)	as far as, up to, until	Noël (m)	Christmas
faux/sse (adj)	false			nord (m)	north
fête (f)	party	là (adv)	there	normalement (adv)	usually
fille (f)	girl	langue (f)	language	notre/nos (possessive adj)	our
fils (m)	boy	leçon (f)	lesson		
fils/fille unique	only child	leur/leurs (possessive adj)	their	nous (personal pronoun)	we
finalement (adv)	finally				
finir	to finish	leur (pronoun)	(to) them	nouveau/nouvelle (adj)	new
fois (f)	time, une fois = once, deux fois = twice	libre (adj)	free		
		lire	to read	nul/le (adj)	rubbish, nothing
		livre (m)	book	offrir	to give (a present)
français (adj)	French	livre (f)	pound (in UK money), pound (in weight)	on (personal pronoun)	'one', we, they, people in general
francophone (adj)	French-speaking				
francophonie (f)	the French-speaking world			ou (conjunction)	or
		loin (adv)	far	où (prep)	where
frère (m)	brother	lui (pronoun)	(to) him	ouest (m)	West
gagner	to earn, to win	lycée (m)	grammar school, sixth-form college	Pâques (f)	Easter
gallois (adj)	Welsh			par (prep)	by, each, per
garçon (m)	boy	magasin (m)	shop	par exemple	for example
se garder en forme	to keep fit and healthy	maintenant (adv)	now	parce que	because
		mais (conjunction)	but	parfois (adv)	sometimes
gâteau (m)	cake	mal (m)	evil, hurt, harm	parler	to speak
gazon (m), hockey sur gazon	lawn, (field) hockey (not ice)	mal (adj)	bad, wrong	partir	to leave
		malheureux/se (adj)	unhappy	pas mal	not bad
général (adj)	general	manger	to eat	passe-temps (m)	pastime, hobby
genre (m)	sort, type, kind	marque (f)	trademark, label	passer	to spend (time), to take (an exam)
gens (m pl)	people	marrant (adj)	funny		
gentil/le (adj)	kind	matière (f)	subject	passionant (adv)	exciting
grave (adj)	serious, deep	le matin	(in the) morning	pays (m)	country
gros/se (adj)	big, fat	mauvais (adj)	bad	pays de Galles (m)	Wales
habillé (adj)	elegant	mèl (m)	email	pendant (prep)	during
s'habiller	to get dressed				

pénible (adj) hard, tiresome, unbearable

un peu a little, a bit

on peut 'one' can, people can, we can, they can

peut-être (adv) perhaps

phoque (m) seal

le/la pire the worst (thing)

plat (m) course (at dinner), dish

plus … que more … than

le plus the most

plus tard later

plusieurs (adj + pronoun) several

portable (m) mobile phone OR laptop computer

porter to wear

pour (prep) for, in order to

pourquoi why/because

pouvoir to be able to, 'can', 'may'

préféré (adj) favourite

préférer to prefer

premier/première (adj) first

prendre to take

près/près de (prep) near

presque (adv) nearly

prochain (adj) next

à la prochaine see you soon!

(au) printemps (m) (in) spring

promener to walk

puis (adv) then

quand when

que what, that

qu'est-ce que … ? what is …?

quel/le which

quelque chose something

quelquefois sometimes

quelqu'un someone

qui who, which

quoi what

raid (adj) straight

ranger to tidy

redoubler (une classe) to repeat a year at school

regarder to watch

remercier to thank

rendre visite à to visit (a person)

rester to stay

rien (pronoun) nothing

romanche (m) a language spoken in parts of Switzerland

sale (adj) dirty

sain (adj) healthy

sans (prep) without

sauf (prep) except (for)

savoir to know

scolaire (adj) school (adjective)

selon (prep) according to

semaine (f) week

seulement (adv) only

si (conjunction) if, whether

site (m) website

sœur (f) sister

(le) soir (in the) evening

soirée (f) party, evening 'do'

sommaire (f) summary

son/sa/ses (possessive adj) his, her, its

sonnerie (f) ringtone

sortir to leave

sous (prep) under

souvent (adv) often

stage (m) (training) course

sud (m) south

sur (prep) on

sûr (adj) sure

surtout (adv) especially, above all

tard (adv) late

techno (f) informal word for technology

de temps en temp from time to time

temps libre (m) free time

titre (m) title

ton/ta/tes (possessive adj) your

tôt (adv) early

toujours (adv) always

tout (adj) all, every

tout ça all that

tout le monde everyone

pas de tout not at all

travail (m) work

travailler to work

travaux manuels (m pl) practical work

tréma (m) two dots placed over a vowel to indicate that it is sounded separately, as in 'naïve'

très (adv) very

triste (adj) sad

troisième (adj) third

trouver to find

trop (adv) too

tu (personal pronoun) you (informal)

tu sais you know

vacances (f pl) holidays

il vaut mieux it would be better to

venir to come

vers (adv) toward, about

vie (f) life

vieux/vieille (adj) old

ville (f) town

voilà there

voir to see

votre/vos (possessive adj) your

je voudrais I would like (to)

vouloir to want (to)

vous (personal pronoun) you (formal or plural)

vrai (true) true

vraiment (adv) really

wolof (m) language spoken in West Africa

y (pronoun) there

zèbre (m) zebra

Grammar index

accent (page 11) A mark above some vowels (or under the letter c) to show a change in pronounciation.

adjective (page 13) A word describing a **noun**, e.g. 'big', 'small', 'stupid', 'honest'.

adjectival agreement (page 13) All **adjectives** in French have to agree with the **noun** they are describing. This means that the noun and the adjective have to match. A **feminine singular** noun needs a feminine singular adjective. When you look up an adjective in a dictionary, it will usually be in the **masculine** singular form, so you might have to change the ending if you use it with **feminine** and/or **plural** nouns.

adverb A word usually describing a **verb**, such as 'I speak French **well**'. In English, adverbs usually end in -ly; in French they usually end in -ment.

article, definite/indefinite See **determiner**.

auxiliary verb (page 33 and 38) A **verb** which can be used with other verbs as a 'helper'. In French, the main auxiliary verbs are *avoir* and *être*, e.g. 'j'**ai** mangé' = 'I **have** eaten'.

cognate (page 43) Words which have identical (or very close) spelling and meaning in both French and English, e.g. *le chocolat* = chocolate.

conditional (page 146) A conditional sentence is one in which one thing depends upon another, often containing the word 'would' in English, e.g. 'I would help you, if I could'.

conjugation 'To conjugate' means to list the various forms of a verb. **Regular** verbs in French belong to one of three groups or conjugations. Their endings are:

		First conjugation	Second conjugation	Third conjugation
Infinitive		-er (e.g. donner)	-ir (e.g. finir)	-re (e.g. attendre)
Present tense	je	-e	-is	-s
	tu	-es	-is	-s
	il/elle/on	-e	-it	-
	nous	-ons	-issons	-ons
	vous	-ez	-issez	-ez
	ils/elles	-ent	-issent	-ent
Past participle		-é	-i	-u
Imperfect	je/tu	-ais	-ais	-ais
	il	-ait	-ait	-ait

connective A word or phrase linking clauses or sentences, e.g. 'and', 'but' or 'first of all'.

determiner Words used with nouns, e.g. 'this', 'my', 'the', 'which'. In French, determiners include definite articles (le, la, les), indefinite articles (un, une, des), **possessive adjectives**, **quantifiers** and some **question words**.

direct object (page 75) See **subject** and **object**.

feminine See **gender**.

future tense (page 143 and 145) See **tense**.

gender (page 18) In French, all nouns belong to one of two groups, either feminine or masculine. (This does not literally mean they are men or women.) You need to know the gender of a noun, so you can use the correct form of the **determiner** or **agreement**.

imperative (page 9, 10) A form of a **verb** used to give commands or instructions.

imperfect tense (page 82) See **tense**.

indirect object (page 139) See **subject** and **object**.

infinitive (page 94) The base form of a **verb**, before it changes to form a particular **tense**. When you look up a verb in a dictionary it will usually be in the infinitive form. Infinitives in English begin with 'to'. All French infinitives end in -er, -ir or -re (see **conjugation**).

interrogative pronoun (page 141) A word used to begin a question such as 'who?', 'what?', 'when?' etc. (Questions can also be formed without an interrogative pronoun; see page 36.)

irregular When the forms of **verbs** and **adjectives** do not follow the normal rules or patterns, they are said to be 'irregular'. Irregular patterns, such as the verb *être* (to be) and the adjective *blanc* (white) need to be learnt by heart.

lower case Letters/words which are not written as capitals or upper case, e.g. UPPER CASE and lower case.

masculine See **gender**.

noun A word used to name something or somebody, e.g. 'chocolate', 'Julie', 'Bradford'.

object See **subject** and **object**.

participle (page 65) The past participle in English often ends in -ed. In French, the past participle is used with an **auxiliary verb**, *avoir* or *être*, to form the perfect **tense**. In both French and English, past participles can be used as **adjectives**.

partitive article (page 113) A type of **determiner** used to say 'some' (du, de, des).

perfect tense (page 65) See **tense**.

person The first person refers to yourself: 'I', 'we'.
The second person refers to the person you are speaking or writing to: 'you'.
The third person refers to somebody or something you are writing about: 'he', 'she', 'it', 'they'.
First, second and third person are subdivided into **singular** and **plural**.

	singular	plural
first person	je (I)	nous (we)
second person	tu (you, informal)	vous (formal or plural)
third person	il (he/it), elle (she/it), on (one)	ils (they), elles (they)

possessive adjective (page 33) In English, words such as 'my', 'your', 'his', 'her', 'its', 'our' and 'their' are used to show that a person or thing is related or belongs to another, e.g. 'my brother', 'her hat'.

preposition (page 39) Words such as 'at', 'with', 'to', 'between', which are usually followed by a **noun** phrase. They often describe the position of something or someone.

present tense (page 52, 60) See **tense**.

pronoun (page 35, 91, 93, 114) A word often used to replace a noun. There are several different types of pronoun:
Personal pronouns (I, he, she, it we, you, they)
Reflexive pronouns (I washed myself)
Relative pronouns (who, that).

quantifier (page 92) Words such as 'quite', 'very', 'a lot' and 'too' are used to make a description more accurate. (Not the same as quantities; see page 112.)

question word (page 141) See **interrogative pronoun**

reflexive verb (page 80) A **verb** which has an extra **pronoun** before it, e.g *se laver* (to wash **oneself**); *je me lave* (I wash **myself**).

regular When the forms of **verbs** and **adjectives** follow the normal rules, they are said to be 'regular'.

scan (page 55) To look over a text quickly, trying to find a key word. See **skim** also.

singular and plural (page 37) Singular forms refer to one thing or person: the book, my sister. Plural forms refer to two or more things or people: the books, my sisters. **Verbs**, **pronouns** and **determiners** often have different singular and plural forms.

skim (page 55) To read so as to get an initial overview of the contents and main points of a text. See **Scan** also.

subject and object (page 75 and 139) In the sentence, 'Julie ate the chocolate', 'Julie' is the subject (the noun performing the action), and 'chocolate' is the object (the noun having the action done to it).
Some sentences can have two objects: Julie gave the **chocolate** to her **friend**. Here 'chocolate' is the direct object (what she gave), and 'her friend' is the indirect object (the person receiving the direct object).

tense A tense is a **verb** form that indicates the time when something happens, in the past, present or future. The present tense describes things happening now or continuously ('I eat chocolate', 'I am eating chocolate').
The perfect tense describes something that happened or has happened in the past ('I ate chocolate', 'I have eaten chocolate').
The imperfect tense describes something that used to happen or was happening in the past ('I used to eat chocolate', 'I was eating chocolate').
The future tense describes something that will happen ('I will eat chocolate').

verb A verb is a word expressing an action or state, a 'doing' or 'being' word. In the sentence, 'Julie is hungry and wants to eat chocolate', 'is', 'wants' and 'to eat' are all verbs.